Easy Bhagavad Gita

A Translation in Simple English

By

Maharudra Chakraborty

Easy Bhagavad Gita

Copyright © Maharudra Chakraborty

All rights reserved. No part of this publication may be reproduced, distributed, or transmitted in any form or by any means, including photocopying, recording, or other electronic or mechanical methods, without the prior written permission of the publisher, except in the case of brief quotations embodied in critical reviews and certain other noncommercial uses permitted by copyright law.

First Edition: 2019
Ebook Also Available

JOLPIC PUBLICATION

For any suggestion mail at: *cmaharudra@gmail.com*

To

The Supreme Entity

Preface

Bhagavad Gita is one of the most celebrated sacred scriptures in Hinduism. More appropriately, someone can also say, the Bhagavad Gita a small part of the vast Hindu scripture Mahabharata. It is the ultimate knowledge that was delivered to Arjuna just before the start of Mahabharata war by lord Krishna. It consists of eighteen chapters and seven hundred verses in total. Each chapter has its own essence. If someone can consume the full knowledge of Bhagavad Gita, and leads his life accordingly, no doubt, his life will be easier than before. It is the key to ultimate success in life.

There are numerous other translations also available in the market. But there is a problem. Since it was originally written in an obsolete language Sanskrit, other authors tried to translate it maintaining the exact grammar and exact depiction of English words from Sanskrit. As a result, it becomes very difficult to understand for common people. The same is true when you try to read Bhagavad Gita in your mother language also. Thus, the final result is that you are able to half understand this book, and the other half remain beyond your realization.

This translation is made a very easy way in English language, so that even children can understand it. This book is written in a storytelling way, thus you will not feel any pressure in your mind while reading it, and you will be able to understand the whole book perhaps for the first time. This book is even easier than those translations in your mother language.

Moreover, this book is not only a religious book. It is a philosophy of life which is needed to know everyone in the world irrespective to his religion. The Bhagavad Gita has the answers to the following questions:

- *How to do work efficiently?*
- *Why do people suffer in their lives?*
- *How to get escape from the sufferings in life?*

- *How to control your mind?*
- *How to concentrate your mind on any subject?*
- *How to achieve liberation?*
- *How to gain knowledge?*
- *What is the ultimate goal in life?*
- *How to lead a happy and peaceful life?*
- *How to get satisfaction in life?*
- *How to attain success?*
- *How to become a good human being?*

And there are many more solutions for your life that you are searching for.

I hope you will become a different person when you will finish this book.

Thank you.

Author

Contents

Prologue   *1*

Chapter One: Arjuna's Lament   *7*

Chapter Two: Self-Realization   *13*

Chapter Three: Laws of Actions   *23*

Chapter Four: Renunciation of Action through Knowledge   *29*

Chapter Five: Renunciation of Actions   *35*

Chapter Six: Practicing Self-Control   *40*

Chapter Seven: The Path of Knowledge and Judgement	*47*
Chapter Eight: The Way to the Eternity	*51*
Chapter Nine: The Secret and Mysterious Knowledge	*56*
Chapter Ten: Endless Glories and Divinities of the Supreme	*61*
Chapter Eleven: Visioning the Supreme	*67*
Chapter Twelve: The Path of Devotion	*75*
Chapter Thirteen: Relation of the Soul to the Body and Nature	*79*
Chapter Fourteen: The Three Qualities	*85*
Chapter Fifteen: The Supreme Entity	*90*
Chapter Sixteen: Demonic and Godlike Personalities	*94*
Chapter Seventeen: Way of Life	*98*
Chapter Eighteen Liberation and Renunciation	*103*

Prologue

Before you start to read the Bhagavad Gita, you need to understand its philosophy, otherwise, you will get confused while reading the book. So, read carefully this chapter before going to the next.

There exists the supreme entity, that is known as the *Brahman* (Caution: do not relate with caste system), or *Paramatma,* or *Parameswar* (*Paramatman* in more conventional). It does not have any structure or form. It is the ultimate source of energy. It is true infinity. It is full of divine consciousness. It is known as the supreme god of Hinduism.

A very good definition of *Paramatma* has been cited in *Isha Upanisad,* which says,
"*Om purnnamdah purnnamidam puurnnaat purnnamudacyate*

Purnnashya purnnamadaaya purnnamevashissyate ||
Om Shaanti Shaanti Shaanti ||"

Its meaning is,

"Aum! It (Brahman or Paramatma) is infinite and purely infinite.
The infinite emerges from the infinite.
Taking away an infinite amount from that infinite,
It remains as the infinite.
Aum, Peace! Peace! Peace!"

Paramatma is like the ocean, if you take away some amount of water from it, it will remain the ocean. The ocean is infinite. We can understand it mathematically; if you subtract infinity from infinity, the answer will always be infinity.

Although it has no structural manifestation according to the definition, we will represent it with a structure in order to understand the full concept. Suppose, the following circle is the structure-less god or the *Paramatma*.

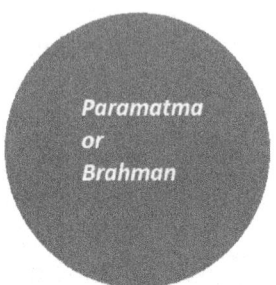

Then some smaller parts come out from the *Paramatma*, these are called the *Atman* (souls). These are the souls in our bodies. These are the reason for the consciousness of all creatures on the earth (or in the other planets, if possible). These are like some water drops has been taken away from the ocean.

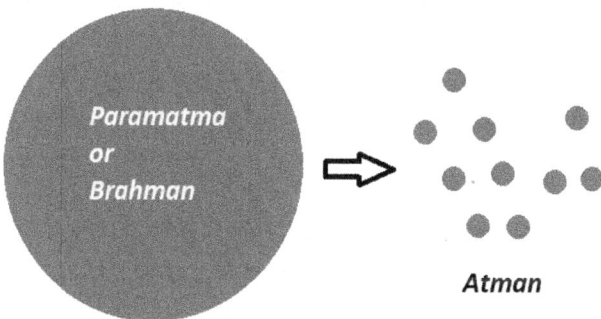

Then those *Atmans* enter to the *Prakriti*.

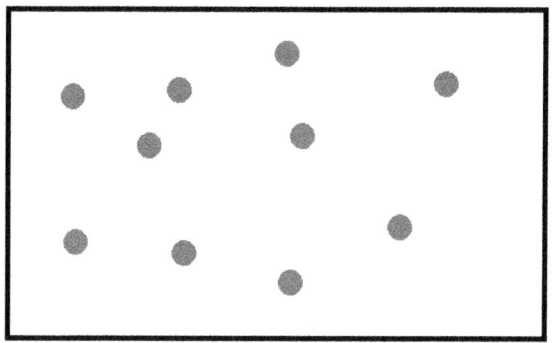

Prakriti

The *Prakriti* (nature) is nothing but our universe. We are living in it. It is the material world, that is made of atoms and molecules, electrons, protons and neutrons. When an *Atman* or a soul enters to the *Prakriti*, it finds a body and takes birth. All the living creatures, from plants to humans, have their own

Atman (soul). Then those living bodies experience pains and comforts, joys and sorrows, all types of other feelings in their lifetime. They show desires for material things, they show anger, they show jealousy and many more. And ultimately they die after a certain period of time. But the story does not end here. After the death, their souls (*Atman*) leave their bodies and again these *Atmans* find new bodies and take birth again. This is the cycle of lives and deaths of an *Atman*, and it will go on.

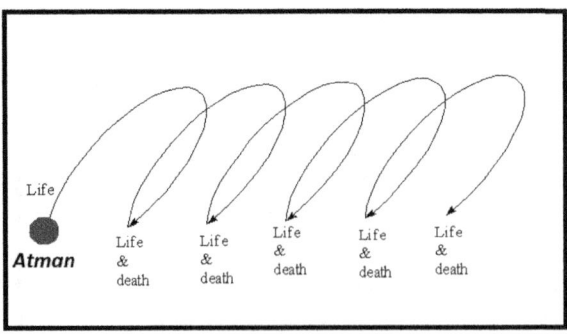

Cycles of lives and deaths of an *Atman* inside *Prakriti*

According to the philosophy of Bhagavad Gita, the *Prakriti* is not a real place, it is an illusion to us. It is like another dimension in a sci-fi movie. It is like a computer simulation where atoms and molecules are the pixels, and someone from the outside operating that computer. Here, all the living creatures are bounded by material things, and they suffer from pains. For that reason, the *Prakriti* is sometime called the *Maya* (illusion or virtual world).

The process of lives and deaths will continue, and an *Atman* will take many reincarnations during the whole process. The *Atmans* will take many births, lives after lives to the forms of many organisms, such as trees, amoeba, fishes, insects, dogs, cats, humans, birds etcetera. One single entity will determine which lifeform an *Atman* will take; it is its own *Karma*.

But, this cannot be a happy ending. An endless cycle of lives and deaths is very much undesirable for an *Atman*; it should have to get escape from the bond of that virtual world. But, how? Bhagavad Gita says that *Atmans* with extraordinary Karmic balance can remove the threshold of its bondage from *Maya*, and finally it can return back to its origin, to the *Brahman*. This meeting with the supreme god is known as *Moksha*.

Every souls or *Atman* is the small parts of the supreme god, the *Brahman* (Paramatma). Due to the reason, every creature can be considered to be as a god itself – not its body but its soul.

The purpose of life is simple. One should have to try to maintain a good karmic balance so that his/her soul can return back to the *Paramatma* at the end of the present life.

Bhagavad Gita is the instruction through which someone gets his liberation from this sorrowful world.

*****

Out of the content, but it is worth to mention one more item. Like the cycle of birth and death of an *Atman*, the universe also has its own process of creation and collapse. The universe is also cyclically created and destroyed after a certain period of time – indeed a very long period. Todays' science also accepts the fact that the universe is a cycle of the big bang and big crunch but it had been already told in the ancient scriptures of Hinduism.

Chapter One
Arjuna's Lament

The war between *Kauravas* (the hundred sons of *Dhritarashtra*) and *Pandavas* (sons of Pandu) was about to start in a few moments on the sacred battlefield of *Kurukshetra*. All the armies were neatly assembled with urges to do battle. No one knew who would win or who would lose, but they were ready to die for the throne.

In the meantime, in the castle of *Hastinapur*, king *Dhritarashtra* asked Sanjay, what my sons and the *Pandavas* did gathering on the holy field of *Kurukshetra*.

Being a blind king, he could not take part in the battle, however, he was able to know what was happening on the battlefield with the help of the narrator Sanjay. *Dhritarashtra* was too affectionate to judge all the sins of his sons. If he could judge his sons, the *Kurukshetra* war never happened.

A special power of distant vision was given to Sanjay by *Vedavyasha* (the author of Mahabharata), through which he was able to see all the happenings in that war and narrated to the king. It was like someone was observing a live cricket match on television, sitting at his home.

Sanjay replied, "your eldest son, king *Duryodhana*, observing the arrangement of armies of the enemy group, went to his preceptor *Dronachrya* and said the following:

"Please observe the army-arrangement of our enemy, it contains many brave and mighty warriors like five *Pandavas*. It has been arranged by your disciple, the son of *Dhrupad, Dhrishtadyumna*. It contains *Satyaki, Yuyudhana, Virata, Drupada, Dhrishtaketu, Chekitana*, the ruler of *Kasi, Purujit, Kuntibhoja, Saivya, Yudhamanyu, Uttamaujas*. It also contains *Subhadra's* son *Abhimanyu*, and five sons of *Draupadi* – they are all mighty cart warriors."

Duryodhana continued, "However our army also contains great warriors like you (*Dronachrya*), *Bhishma, Kripachrya, Ashwathhama, Bikarna*, and *Somdatta's* son *Bhurishrava*. Besides them, there are many soldiers who are ready to die for me in this battle - they all are heroic warriors."

"Our army is being well preserved by my great-warrior grandfather *Bhishma*, thus, we are almost undefeatable by *Pandavas*. Whereas, their army is easily defeatable by us because their army is being protected by *Bhima*."

"So, you are requested to protect *Bhishma* with your all strength, and arrange your army to accomplish that intention."

Then, the brave warrior *Bhishma* loudly roared like a lion with intense joy, creating fearlessness in *Duryodhana's* heart. All the conchs, drums, tabors, trumpets were played at that moment to announce the beginning of the battle.

Simultaneously, Arjuna and his chariot driver lord Krishna blew their own conch shells. The chariot of Arjuna was given by *Indra*, the god of thunder, and it was pulled seven white horses. Lord Krishna blew his *Panchajanya*, *Bhim* blew *Poundra*, *Judhisthir* blew *Anantavijay*, *Nakul* blew *Sughosha* and *Sahadev* blew *Manipuspaka* conch shells.

King of Kashi, warrior *Shikhandi*, king *Virata*, *Satyaki*, king *Dhrupada*, five sons of *Pandavas*, and *Abhimanyu* blew their own conch shells. The enormous sound of those conch shells was so powerful that it shivered the sinful king *Duryodhana's* heart. The powerful sound seemed to tremble the heaven and the earth.

Thereafter, Arjuna, sitting on his chariot, observed the opponent army and discovered there are many relatives of him wishing for battle. He raised his hand, holding his *Gandiva* bow, and ordered lord Krishna, "O Krishna, please place my chariot in between both armies. I am wishing to properly observe those war seeking people, and I have to decide with whom I have to do war."

Arjuna continued, "I want to observe all the enemies who are ready to die for the sinful minded

Duryodhana. They all are the well-wishers of *Duryodhana,* and gathered for the battle."

"Keep my chariot in the middle until I see them all."

Lord Krishna fulfilled Arjuna's wish and he drove the chariot towards the middle of the battlefield. He kept his chariot at the desired position, and said to Arjuna, "See your enemies, the Kauravas."

He carefully observed both the groups of armies, and discovered that both the armies were filled with his brothers, his sons, his grandfathers, his uncles, his in-laws, his friends, his teachers, and all other kinsmen.

Seeing his family members in those armies, his eyes became wet, and a deepest sorrow captured his heart, and said to Krishna, "Dear Krishna, seeing the gatherings of all my family members in this battlefield, my full body is becoming tired, my mouth is drying. I am shivering with sorrow."

"My hands become unable to hold my bow, my skin is burning, I am feeling senseless, I cannot stand still."

"All possible omens are coming in my mind. Thus, I am unable to find any reason to kill my family members in this battleground."

"I don't wish to get a victory. I don't want the happiness of owning the throne. There is no happiness of becoming a king without friends and families."

"We deserve the victory, we deserve happiness, we deserve to be king, merely to fulfil the wishes of our family members. And see, today they all have gathered to do battle quitting their wishes of survival, leaving their wealth, rejecting their intelligence."

"Most of them are my teachers, my sons, my brothers, my cousins, my uncles, my friends, and all other relatives. They are relatives of our relatives. If they wish to kill me on the battlefield, I would not fight with them. I am unable to use my weapons to them."

"If someone offers me the whole earth, heavens and all the possible happiness and wealth in this universe, yet I could not kill them"

"What happiness would I deserve by killing those *Kauravas*? Rather, there will be a sin if I kill them."

"Although, they are not finding any sin because their minds get ruined by their greediness. However, we should not, we are already aware of the evil coming from the extinction of a family."

"When heirs of a family become extinct, the deepest sin outbreaks among all other families."

"If evils flow towards other families, the women of those families become corrupt. Ultimately, the evils will cause the intermixture of castes."

"Intermixture of castes leads their ancestors to hell. Also who were the killers of those families, they will be also put into hell."

"Alas! In spite of being intelligent, we are ready to do the same greatest sin. It will be better for me, if *Dhritarashtra's* sons kill me in this battleground, when I am being unarmed and not defending myself, with a wish of not killing them."

Arjuna's mind was occupied with lamentation. After all, Kauravas were his brothers, the sons of his uncle. However, Kauravas felt extremely jealousy at Pandavas and they had their sinful minds. So, they did not do the good justice towards Pandavas, rather tortured them in many ways. The ultimate fate was a great war. That was the war of Kurukshetra.

Many kings took part in this war, and expectedly, there would have many deaths. Arjuna was aware of many spilling of blood. Being a sentimental person, he felt the sorrow and told about his feelings to his close friend Krishna.

He was reluctant to do war and still remained inactive for the war, sitting on his chariot, keeping his weapons aside.

Chapter Two
Self-Realization

Arjuna was not willing to pick up his weapon anymore. His eyes were full of tears. The deepest grief of losing his family had been established in his mind. He remained silent until Krishna spoke his words to him.

Lord Krishna said, "How such delusion came to your head, in in the wrong place, at the wrong time? Great persons do not act like that, and also, it will not lead you to heaven after your death."

"Thus, Dear Arjuna, do not remain inactive. It does not match with your personality. Reject your heart's weakness and rise for the battle."

Arjuna said, "How can I fight with arrows against my grandfather *Bhishma* and my teacher *Dronacharya*? They all are the respectful persons to me."

"Thus, I am unable to battle with those elders, rather it will be more blissful for me if I live the rest of my life with earned alms from begging. The bloodstained wealth earned from slaying those people will be worthless on the earth."

"Dear Krishna, give me a suggestion, which option will be better for me? – will I continue to battle or not?"

"We do not know, who will get the victory. They may defeat us or we may defeat them, still, I do not wish to survive after killing them. However, my family members *Kauravas* eager to do this battle."

"So, my heart is filled with helplessness, my mind deviates from my duties. Still, I am asking you for the righteous suggestions. Considering me as your disciple, show me the proper path."

"I am unable to find any remedy which can remove my pain of losing families, although having the prosperity of being a king."

Thus, Arjuna again remained silent by clearly saying "I shall not engage in the war."

Lord Krishna said with his smiled face, "Dear Arjuna, you are feeling sorrow for those people who do not deserve your grief. Furthermore, you are speaking like a learned person. But the truth is, a wise man never shows lament for any living or dead person."

"It is not true that I or you did not live before. Or, those armies on this battlefield did not live before. Even, it is also true that we are not immortals."

"As the souls in our bodies experience childhood, youth and old age, likewise souls acquire new bodies after death. Sensible persons aware of that truth."

"Dear Arjuna, all the organs in our bodies sense heat and cold, sorrow and happiness, though these senses are not permanent. These will come and go. So, you have to tolerate them."

"Because, those people, who remain equally stable in sorrow and happiness, who did not distract by the connection between the organs and his sufferings, finally achieve the *Moksha* (meet to the Paramatma, the ultimate god of Hinduism)."

"There is no existence for unreal, but there is the existence for real. Our mortal world is unreal and it is only an illusion to us, our souls are real but our bodies are unreal. Wise people aware of the reality of the ultimate truth."

"Only eternal entity is that, by which all the universe is pervaded. No one can destroy that eternal entity."

"When eternal, indestructible and infinite soul forms a body, the body becomes mortal and died. So, dear Arjuna, pick up your bow and arrows, and fight against your opponent."

"Who think that the soul is the slayer of others or the soul can be slain, they are not aware of the truth. The truth is, the soul cannot be killed or it can not kill anyone."

"The soul neither takes birth nor dies at all. It always exists. It is unchangeable, eternal, ancient. A body can die but its soul does not."

"If someone knows that a soul is indestructible, everlasting, unborn, and inexhaustible, how can it kill someone or to be killed by someone?"

"As a person rejects his old clothes and puts on a new one, likewise, a soul leaves an old body and takes a new one."

"No weapon can cut it, fire cannot burn it, water cannot wet it and air cannot dry it. Because it is not divisible, it is not combustible, it is not to be moistened, it is not to be dried up."

"Thus the soul is called the eternal and stable, and knowing that truth, you should not have to feel sorrow."

"If you ever think the soul is not eternal, yet, you should not feel pain. Because, one that is born, death is certain; and to one that dies, birth is certain. So, you should not feel pain."

"All creatures are unrecognizable before birth and become unrecognizable again after death. Only they are recognizable when they are living. – There is no requirement of lamentation."

"Some people know the soul as a wonder, some people describe the soul as a wonder, and some people listen about it as a wonder. However, many people are still not able to understand it, because the soul is beyond humans' knowledge."

"As I said, the soul cannot be killed when it is inside a body, thus, there should not have any reason for sorrow."

"Being a *Kshatriya*, you do not have any other duties except the righteous battle. So, be fearless and concentrate on your duties."

"Dear Arjuna, only a few *Kshatriyas* avail such opportunity to fight this type of heavenly righteous war."

"If you do not fight this battle, you abandon your duties and thus it will be sinful to you."

"You will be considered to be a coward in the upcoming history and everyone will gossip about your cowardliness in the future. For a wise person, infamy is more painful than his death."

"Those people, who show respect you most, will dishonor you and they will think you abandoned the battle due to the fear of death."

"Your enemy will talk about your littleness and your fame will be faded. What can be more lamentable than that?"

"If you are killed in this war, you will go to heaven. And if you get the victory, you will enjoy the earth. Thus, arise and engage in the battle."

"Consider, victory and defeat, gain and loss, joy and sorrow equally and ready for the battle, and thus you will not incur sin."

"Hereby, I declared the Yoga of knowledge for you. Now, listen to the Yoga of action. Thus, gaining that knowledge dear Arjuna, you will be free from the bonds of action."

"Doing action without desire eliminates the obstacles of that action. There will not have any fear of starting that action or fear of opposite results.

Even it eliminates all the fear of mightiest danger such as death."

"Doing action without desire will help to concentrate the mind to that action. But, who are ready to do the action with desire, their minds get diverted towards many uncertainties like the branches of a tree."

"Dear Arjuna, there are many people whose minds are always attached to earthly pleasures and prosperities, who only do their actions to achieve the final desirous result, who always think that reaching to the heaven is the ultimate goal of the entire life. They follow their religious scriptures in order to attain prosperity, lavishness, and heaven. Their minds are attracted to the talk of such actions.

They are not following the right path in their lives. Their thoughts are not pure. Their minds are far away from the thought of Paramatma."

"Religious scriptures are related to three qualities (*Satwva*, *Rajasa* and *Tama*sa) of action, and instruction of these three qualities are provided there. You should reject your attachment towards pleasure and prosperity. Concentrate your mind towards eternal Paramatma, forgetting happiness and sorrow."

"There is no requirement of a small pond if someone achieves the ocean, similarly, there is no requirement of religious scriptures if someone knows the truth, the truth about the eternity of soul and Paramatma."

"You have the authority towards your actions and duties, but not their results. So you should not become the owner of the action's outcome.

However, it does not mean that you should leave your duties."

"Dear Arjuna, leave your all attachment in your life. Every action can have its desired and opposite results, always treat them equally in life. The expected result is not in your hand, so leave any expectation and do your action with ultimate effort."

"Those actions which are done with achieving desired expectations by someone, are of inferior qualities. Those persons who do their action to get the desired results are also inferior qualities.

So, try to accept the success and failure equally of your action, before committing that."

"Wise people always do their work with maintaining this equality of failure and success, and ultimately they become free from the bond of action. They achieve their position beyond sin and merit, above heaven and hell. Their souls become connected directly to the Paramatma. And finally, their souls do not take birth again and meet with the Paramatma, after their deaths."

"You also do the same following their pathways; when you will cross a certain limit refusing the all attachments with mortal pleasures and prosperities, you will experience, all those earthly matters are valueless. Your mind will be stabilized to the thought of Paramatma. A continuous connection will be created between your soul and the Paramatma.

This is the ultimate devotion and you will become a devotee."

Now lord Krishna stopped his speech at that moment, and Arjuna asked him again, "What are the characteristics of those devotees? How do they speak to other persons? How do they behave?"

Krishna replied, "When a devotee abandons all his desires from his mind and stay happy with his soul instead of his body, he is then called a 'steady minded."

"His mind does not fluctuate in happiness and sorrow, anger or fear. He does not attract towards any person or any precious thing; he does not react to good or bad; He does not show jealousy.

As a tortoise shrinks its organs inside its shell, likewise, a steady-minded devotee withdraws his organs from all of the availabilities for his pleasures. Then, he is called a steady-minded sage."

"However, when someone withdraws his organs from self-satisfaction, his organs remained unsatisfied. Thoughts about those pleasures do not become extinct. But, the remaining attractions are nullified when he meets to Paramatma."

"Even, those remaining attractions are the cause of fluctuation of a very intelligent mind. Thus, control your organs from self-pleasures because only those who are able to control their organs, can achieve a steady-minded condition."

"When a mind thinks about its body's pleasure, the thoughts convert to desire. And, when the desire is not fulfilled, it converts to anger.

The anger creates confusion in mind. The confusion is the reason for memory loss. The memory loss creates a loss of intelligence. And, the loss of intelligence ruins that person."

"When a person has learned to control his inner self, no bit of attachment and jealousy can touch him. His inner soul stays always happy.

He may be the owner of an enormous amount of wealth or he may be a poor person, but, neither he feels an attachment to that wealth nor feels sorrow having no wealth. Because, being a steady-minded, his soul connected to the Paramatma.

On the other hand, who does not have the self-control to his organ through his mind, his soul remains unconnected to the Paramatma. He does not get peace in his entire life. And, without peace, there is no happiness."

"The wind can lead a boat towards any directions on a river, similarly, a person's mind can lead his organs to any directions. Thus, his organs are attracted to earthly objects to find his pleasure. And finally, those organs destroy his senses.

Dear Arjuna, who has restrained his organs from earthly pleasures by controlling his mind, practicing that way, his mind becomes steady."

"Those devotees with the self-controlled mind (steady minded) stay awake in the happiness of eternal knowledge. All the attachments with earthly pleasure remain in dark near to them.

Whereas, those people, who stay awake with those earthly pleasures due to the lack of self-controlled minds, the true knowledge remains in the dark for them."

"A river meets to the ocean without agitating its water, similarly, a self-controlled person does not feel any agitation in his mind towards earthly objects for self-pleasure. He achieves the ultimate peace in his life.

But, who is a seeker of earthly pleasure, peace remains beyond their range."

"The person, who is free from any attachment, who is free from egoism, and who is free from proud feeling, achieves peace and he meets to the Paramatma."

"These all are the characteristics of a steady-minded devotee. Once someone has learned to control his mind, he never feels attachment in his lifetime, and when he dies, he meets to the Paramatma."

Chapter Three
Laws of Actions

Arjuna said, "Dear Krishna, you have mentioned that the path of knowledge is superior to the path of action, then why are you insisting me to do such action of killing people.

Your dual words are creating confusion in my mind.

Please show me only one specific path, which will be better for me."

Krishna replied, "Dear Arjuna, as I have said there are two available paths to follow. One is the path of knowledge and another is the path of action. But, both paths are important in life. Knowledge cannot be gained without the path of action, similarly, action cannot be fulfilled without the path of knowledge."

"No one can lead his life without doing any work (action). Every moment people are doing something due to their instinct.

However, those confusing people, who have learned to control their organs, yet they have thought of availing earthly pleasures in their mind, are called liars.

But, who has learned to control his organs with doing actions so that he becomes busy with his works thus other unnecessary thought cannot deviate his mind.

Doing some actions is better than doing no action. So, you should always be busy to do some actions."

"Those actions, which have been accomplished without any intention for good deed, create attachments. So, forgetting any attachment, you should do actions for good."

"After creating this universe, the god created humans. Then he directed them to do good actions because it would create a good effect for them."

"They had been directed to worship god, so that, they can be enriched by god's blessings. It was suggested for their good. The god would deliver the proper results and they would gain prosperity."

"But, who consume their god given wealth without donating to others, they are called thieves.

Who cooks foods for the purpose of his own nutrition, he is actually incurring his sins. Donation of foods can abolish one's sin."

"All the creatures are created from foods; those foods are created from rain; rain is created from good deeds of people, and good deeds are created from the action.

Since laws of actions had been created by Paramatma, good deeds and Paramatma are inherently connected to each other."

"Who refuse to do their actions because of addiction to their own pleasures, it is comparable to their deaths."

"Very few devotees have proper knowledge about their souls. They are happy with their souls; they contend with their souls. They are free from their actions. They have nothing have to do further.

They are so knowledgeable persons that they are not dependent on their actions. They are not bounded to give and take policy with other beings."

"Therefore, dear Arjuna, you should continue to do your actions rejecting all of your attachments. Because, actions, that have been done without any attachment by someone, leads to the path of Paramatma."

"Long time ago, king *Janaka* and other devotees like him did their actions without any desire. So, certainly, they have met the Paramatma."

"You should follow their pathways, doing so, on a later stage, other people will also follow your ideologies.

Because people always follow great and knowledgeable peoples' ideologies. Those wise persons leave their impressions on earth and common people are influenced by their pathways."

"Think about me, I am Krishna, I am the god. There is no action that I have to do; there is nothing that I cannot acquire. In spite of that, I am always busy with doing my actions. I never refuse to do work (action)."

"Dear Arjun, the reason is, if I ever denied to do my actions, it would be harmful to society. Being a supreme person, people will follow my ideologies for many generations.

If I refuse to do my duties, following me, people will also do the same, and as a result, the civilization would be destroyed, and I would become the reason of that abolishment."

"Dear Arjun, as common people do their actions to maintain society, the knowledgeable wise people also do the same. Thus, those wise persons get their followers."

"Those wise people should maintain their continuous flow of actions (for good deeds) such a way that common ignorant people never dishonor them. They should accomplish their actions by themselves and they should also help to fulfill those ignorant peoples' actions with their knowledge."

"All types of actions related to good deeds are accomplished by knowledge, and not by persons. But an ignorant person thinks that he is the sole owner of his actions."

"A knowledgeable person is never attracted to earthly pleasures and prosperities, since he knows the truth that knowledge and action are interrelated. Knowledge is transforming into action, and action is transforming into knowledge."

"The Maya (the illusion of the universe) creates attachments among ignorant people towards their actions. However, wise people should not deviate them from their actions."

"Dear Arjuna, devote all your actions to the Paramatma, and be ready for the battle, forgetting all the desires from your mind."

"People, who follow my ideologies with full devotion and without any sinful thought, get escape from all bounds of their good or bad actions.

But, those people, who blame me every time and disobey my ideologies, are ignorant, and they are following the wrong paths."

"All beings are compelled to do their own actions due to their instinct. Wise people also do their own. But, what if they go against nature and commit sins?"

"All humans have their own anger and jealousy in their subconscious minds. However, those remain inactive until someone is controlled by those evils.

Anger and jealousy are the enemies to the way of self-realization and knowledge."

"Different people have their own different actions in their lives. One's action may be superior to others. Thus, one might realize that his action (or work) is not superior and he might try to copy others. But, it is a very dangerous act for him.

One should follow his own path or action even it is not superior like others. If he dies to do so, it will be better for him than copying others."

Lord Krishna paused and Arjuna asked him again, "Dear Krishna, why do people commit sins? What are the reasons for their unwillingly or forcefully committed sins? Who is driving and compelling them to do so?"

"Some qualities inherent to a person create desire and anger in his mind. These two are very hungry and their hunger cannot be suppressed by any means. If someone tries to suppress these by wealth and pleasure, these increase more. These two are evil enemies for all."

"As smoke covers fire, dust covers a mirror, a womb covers its embryo, similarly, the desire covers all the knowledge.

Desire is the enemy of a wise person. It is hungry like fire. As fire increases by fuel, desire increases by its desirous objects. Knowledge is covered by desire."

"The desire takes shelter in the mind, organ, and senses and manipulate them in order to cover up knowledge. Thus, the soul is bounded to attachments."

"You need to control your organ first to destroy your all desires."

"Organs are superior to the body; the mind is superior to organs; Sense is superior to mind. But the soul is far superior to sense."

"Knowing the fact that the soul is greatest to all, using your senses, control your mind. Then, destroy all the desires within you."

Chapter Four
Renunciation of Action through Knowledge

Lord Krishna stated, "Long time ago, I declared this eternal path of devotion to the sun god, then he transferred it to his son, Manu; and thereafter, Manu transferred it to his son, king Ishkvaku.

Dear Arjuna, many kings and their descendants had been enlightened through this path. But, it had been faded away by time."

"Since you are my disciple and friend, I also stated this secret and mysterious path of devotion to you."

Arjuna said, "Dear Krishna, the sun and those kings were born in ancient time, but you are recent. Then, how can I understand that you declared it to them?"

Krishna said, "Dear Arjuna, you and me had been passed through many incarnations (births) in the past. You forgot them, but I remember."

"I am unborn; I am immortal; I am the supreme god. Still, I take birth as a human and live among them.

Whenever the decline of good and outbreak of evil occur on the earth, I reincarnate myself.

I come to the earth to protect the good people and to destroy the evil doers. I reestablish the holiness again on this earth."

"My birth and actions are pure and spiritual. Who knows me completely and devote himself to me, he never has to take his birth again, and he meets me (Paramatma) after his death."

"Whose minds are completely free from any fear, anger, and attachment, who completely devoted to me, are able to know me completely. Many divine devotees like them attained the place of my true self."

"Dear Arjun, as people show their devotions to me in their own ways, I reward them following the same ways. Because all people are unknowingly or knowingly following my paths."

"People, who desirously do their action, worship demigods. Because they readily get their fruitful results."

"I created the division of four classes of people according to their actions and qualities. Being the supreme god, and being eternal, I am the creator of all creations, but you should know me to be the non-doer (inaction).

Since I have no desire for the fruit of my action, any action is not able to bind me. The person who knows me that way, is also never bounded by his actions.

Knowing this, many previous devotees did their actions without any desire. You should also follow the same and do your action accordingly."

"Action and inaction are different. Even sensible wise persons are not able to differentiate them properly. I am describing you all of their features for your awareness. If you understand them properly, you will be able to be free from evils and bound of your actions.

There are three types of actions, these are action, inaction and forbidden action. Everyone should know their proper meanings, because the 'law of action' is difficult to understand."

"Those persons are known as wise, sage and knowledgeable, who perform all his actions and they see action in their inactions and inactions in their actions.

Those people are known as learned, who perform their actions without any desire. Their all actions (good or bad) thus have been consumed by the fire of their knowledge."

"Those persons, who find their peace through the thinking of Paramatma, leaving all their actions and desires in life, they refused the shelter of any comfort, are free from the effect of their action. If they continue their actions, those actions are considered to be as inaction."

"Those people, whose minds and organs are perfectly controlled, and who rejected all the material things for their pleasures, are free from the bound of their actions. They only do their actions for their survivals and livings, thus, their actions are not to be considered as sinful (inaction)."

"Those people, who become happy what they are getting spontaneously for their living, who are free from jealousy, who are free from happiness and sorrow, who are free from failure and success, do their actions only for their living, and those actions are considered to be the inaction."

"Those people, who are free from desire, who do nothing to get their comfort, whose minds are filled with the thoughts of Paramatma, who only do their actions for the purpose of sacrifice to the god, are the person of inaction. Their actions are not to be counted for their karmic balance."

"Who sacrifice everything to the Paramatma, his all actions are also unknowingly sacrificed to the Paramatma. Their actions do not affect their karmic balance (inaction). Thus they achieve the ultimate results reaching to the Paramatma."

"Different people find their own ways of sacrifice. Some people perform sacrifice by worshipping gods. Some people consider the fire as an image of the supreme Paramatma and sacrifice into it."

"Some people perform sacrifice by controlling their organs. Some people sacrifice their actions, enlightening them by knowledge. Some people sacrifice through self-controlling themselves."

"Some people sacrifice by donating to poor people. Some people sacrifice by penance. Some people sacrifice by performing nonviolence. Some people sacrifice by taking vows. Some people sacrifice by self-illuminating themselves. Some people sacrifice by performing breathing exercise. Some people sacrifice by limited intake of foods. Some people sacrifice by meditation. They certainly know the true meaning of sacrifice."

"The act of the performance of sacrifice will lead them to the Paramatma. But, who do not sacrifice, their lives become misery in this world and also in the world after death."

"Many other ways of sacrifices have been described in the sacred literatures. Those all are performed by the mind, senses, organs, and actions. Dear Arjuna, performing those sacrifices, you will be able to renounce from the attachments to your actions."

"Dear Arjuna, the sacrifices that are done for gaining knowledge is superior to the sacrifices performed by material things. Because all the actions are ended up by gaining knowledge."

"Dear Arjuna, you can gain your knowledge from those knowledgeable people. They will enlighten you by their knowledge when you ask them with your pure mind."

"Enlightened by knowledge, you will be no longer bound by any attachment. The knowledge will show you the true nature of your soul, and you will be able to realize your true-self. Then, you will be able to realize the Paramatma who is inside me."

"If you would be the most sinful than all sinners, you will able to escape from the ocean of sin by the boat of your knowledge."

"Because, dear Arjuna, as the fire burns all its fuels, similarly, knowledge burns all the actions."

"There is nothing in this world as pure as knowledge. When the mind becomes pure with long practicing of actions (without desire), knowledge enlightens the mind automatically."

"Only self-controlled, respectful devotees can gather that knowledge, and they attain the ultimate spiritual peace."

"On the other hand, ignorant, faithless people become diverted from the path of knowledge. Those doubtful people do not have happiness in this life and afterlife."

"Who have already sacrificed all their actions to the Paramatma, and eliminated all the doubts by their senses, actions are not able to bind them at all."

"Thus, dear Arjuna, you should abolish your all doubts by the sword of your knowledge. And be ready for the battle."

Chapter Five
Renunciation of Actions

Arjuna said, "Dear Krishna, you mentioned that both the path, 'renunciation of actions' and 'actions without desire' are valuable in life. Kindly show me the exact path which will be more beneficial for me."

Lord Krishna said, "Both of the paths in life are useful, but the path of actions without desire is superior to the renunciation of actions, and it is easier to follow."

"People, who do not jealous of others, who do not keep desire in their mind, are called the sages (wise and knowledgeable). The always do their actions without any desire, and hence, they are easily released from this earthly world (they attain the Moksha)."

"Ignorant people say that these two paths yield distinct results, but wise people do not say the same. Because, wise people know, choosing any of them will lead to the Paramatma."

"Both the followers of these two paths attain the same place after their deaths. So, a knowledgeable person always treats these two paths equally."

"Dear Arjuna, it is nearly impossible to follow the path of renunciation of actions without following the path of action. Since, rejection of all actions done by mind, organs, and body is extremely hard. But, the path of action without desire is relatively easier to follow, and it also can provide the same result of attaining the Paramatma."

"Those people, whose minds and organs are well controlled, whose senses are pure, who have identified every living being as a part of the Paramatma (soul), are the knowledgeable people. Those people do not have any bond to their actions (their actions are inactions)."

"Those knowledgeable persons, who are practicing the path of renunciation of actions through their knowledge, consider that their organs are automatically doing their actions such as seeing, listening, smelling, eating, moving, sleeping, breathing, talking, excreting, taking, eyes' blinking etc. and their minds think that they are doing nothing."

"Who dedicate all their actions to the Paramatma, and do their actions without attachment, they are not touched by any sin, like water drops on a lotus leaf."

"Those people, who are practicing the path of actions without desire, do their actions to achieve the purification of the mind by rejecting all attachments towards their organs, minds, senses, and bodies."

"These people, who are practicing the path of action with no desire, attain peace towards Paramatma through the rejection of the outcome of actions.

Whereas, the people with desires attract towards the fruit (result) of their actions."

"With self-controlled minds and senses, wise people reject all actions and inactions through their senses and concentrate their minds to the Paramatma.

Because the supreme Paramatma does not create any attachment towards the outcome of actions in the human mind, however, the attachments are created by the habits of people.

The supreme Paramatma does not take any sin or good deed from anyone, but his mind creates attachments because his ignorance covers up all his knowledge."

"When ignorance has been destroyed by the illuminating knowledge, the knowledge then shines the Paramatma like the sun."

"Whose minds, senses and faiths are completely devoted to Paramatma, they ultimately get escape from all their sins through the knowledge and attaining the place to the Paramatma, they never take rebirth again (Moksha)."

"Realizing the truth that souls are the true identity of all creatures, a knowledgeable wise person equally behaves with all living creatures, such as humans, cows, elephants, dogs etc.

Whose mind is stable with such equanimity, has already attained his deserved position while living on the earth. Because, the supreme being, Paramatma is pure and filled with similar equanimity, so his soul has also earned its rewarded position."

"A stable and doubtless minded sage never expresses joy after getting a pleasant object, likewise, he never expresses regret after getting an unpleasant object. Such person's soul has achieved its place to the Paramatma.

He is unattached towards any earthly pleasure, and he finds his joy only with his eternal soul. Devoting himself to the Paramatma, he achieves his peace."

"Wealth and prosperity bring happiness to a person for a limited period of time. But, those are the reason for the sadness also. These earthly pleasures are not eternal, thus dear Arjuna, a sensible person never attaches to them."

"Just before someone's death, people fail to tolerate the impulse coming from their angers and desires. Thus, happiest devotees are those, who easily tolerate the ultimate destiny of life."

"Who is filled with the happiness of his soul, who is filled with knowledge about his soul, he becomes unified with Paramatma, achieving the Moksha."

"Whose all sins have been abolished, whose all doubts have been cleared through enlightening knowledge, who is always busy to do work for others' wellness, whose mind is calm, self-controlled and devoted to the Paramatma – he is the deserved person, who will ultimately achieve his liberation."

"The person, who is free from any anger and desire, whose mind is self-controlled, who becomes knowledgeable by enlightening his mind with the Paramatma, is surrounded by the divine Paramatma in his all directions."

"The devotee, who practices meditation rejecting all his desires from his mind, concentrating his vision between his two eyebrows, controlling his breathing through his nostrils, stabilizing his mind and senses, abolishing all his desires, fearsofand anger, must achieve his liberation towards Paramatma."

"My devotees find their peace knowing me completely. They become aware that I am the ultimate purpose of all their devotions and sacrifices, I am the god of all gods, I am the selfless, affectionate and merciful and I am the well-wisher for all beings."

Chapter Six
Practicing Self-Control

Lord Krishna continued, "Those people are true devotees and wise who perform their duties without expectation, but not those people who abandoned their sacrifices and actions for others' wellness."

"Dear Arjuna, devotions and renunciation are the same, because, nobody becomes a devotee unless he renounced his earthly pleasures."

"The path of action without desire is the primary reason for someone's devotion. When someone performs his act of devotion, he feels no desire to his performed actions and it is indeed a good sign for him."

"When a person does not feel any attachment to his organs' pleasure and to his performed actions, the desire-less person is called a devotee."

"One should try to elevate himself, rather degrading himself. Because a human is a friend and as well as an enemy to himself.

Who is able to control his mind, organs, and body, he becomes a friend for himself. On the other hand, who has not learned it yet, he still remains an enemy for himself."

"Whose mind is stable in hot and cold, in joy and sorrow, in honor and dishonor, his mind is then said to be perfectly devoted to the Paramatma."

"A person becomes a true devotee when his mind becomes satisfied with self-realization and knowledge, when his mind is stabilized and it can control his all organs against desire, when a piece of gold and a piece of stone both become equally valueless to him."

"A person with great mind shows neutrality towards friend and enemy, well-wisher and sinner, selfless and selfish etcetera."

"One should devote himself to the Paramatma by meditating his mind. While he is meditating, his mind should be well balanced through controlling his body and organs, he should renounce all his desires, he should be alone, and the place should be isolated from all disturbances.

The place should be sacred, not to be too high or too low. He should prepare his seat by placing some grasses or deer-skin or clothes."

"Sitting there, he should practice his meditation in order to purify his soul, concentrating his mind, and controlling his organs and body."

"His head, spine, and neck should be straight and steady. He should stare steadily to the tip of his nose with his both eyes. He should not move his eyes and body during the preform of the meditation process."

"His mind should be free from all fears and lusts. He should carefully control his mind and continue the meditation."

"He should devote his soul to me through imagining that I am the image of the supreme Paramatma. Practicing the meditation, he will attain his ultimate peace."

"Dear Arjuna, this process of meditation is not fulfilled for those, who eat too much or eat nothing at all, and who sleep too much or sleep too low."

"The practice of devotion through meditation can only be achieved when someone maintains a balanced food intake and sleeping habit in his lifestyle."

"When someone's mind is completely devoted to the Paramatma through renouncing all the desires of earthly pleasures, the person is then called a devotee."

"As the flame of a candle does not fluctuate in airless place, similarly, a meditating mind can concentrate in the same way without fluctuating."

"Meditation can open a closed mind, thus the mind finds its peace and purity through the devotion to the Paramatma."

"A devotee experiences his ultimate happiness which would not be felt through his organs, but it can only be felt through his mind. Attaining such mental pleasure, his mind does not ever deviate from the thought of Paramatma."

"Achieving the liberation of his soul (achieving the Paramatma), he decides that none is worthier than this. Attaining that stage, he never becomes unstable even in his deepest sorrow."

"Devotion is unattached to the misery of Maya. One should practice the method of meditation regularly with his positive and motivated mind."

"One should practice it renouncing all his desires and self-controlling his organs through his mind."

"Prolonged practice will bring calmness to his mind and senses, so that his mind will be concentrated on the Paramatma."

"A fluctuating mind is always seeking for its desires, but this meditation will not let him think any desirous thought."

"If ever desirous thought comes, his mind will compel him to revert back to the thought of Paramatma due to the good effect of the meditation."

"Having a peaceful and sinless mind with good qualities, a devotee reaches his ultimate pleasure, and becomes united with the Paramatma."

"That virtuous devotee continuously associates his soul to the Paramatma and easily finds his ultimate mental pleasure."

"Connecting his soul to the endless consciousness (Paramatma), the devotee sees his soul in all beings and sees all beings in his souls."

"Who sees everything in me, and sees me in everything, I never disappear to him, and he is not disappeared to me."

"The person, who devotes to me imagining that I am everywhere, he always stays inside me regardless of his behavior."

The greatest devotees are those, who selflessly feels pain in everyone's pain and feels happiness in everyone's happiness."

Arjuna said, "Dear Krishna, the way of meditation, as you described to me, seems to be difficult to implement for an ordinary person. Because, the mind is restless and unsteady, thus the method may not be durable for a long period."

"Human mind is restless, fluctuating and it overpowers to all, so I think that it is impossible to control the mind as like confining the restless wind."

Lord Krishna replied, "Dear Arjuna, doubtlessly, the mind is restless and difficult to control, however, it can be controlled through prolonged practice and renunciation."

"Indeed, this method is extremely difficult for those people who have desires in their minds and lack of self-control. But, a person of self-discipline and self-control definitely can attain this devotion."

Arjuna asked him again, "There are some people who are good devotees, however, their minds are not steady enough. So, it may be possible that before their deaths, their minds get deviated from the state of devotion. As a result, they are unable to meet to the Paramatma. Then where do they go?

Dear Krishna, being deviated from the Paramatma, do their souls decay like fragmented clouds?

Please enlighten me. No one is able to eliminate my doubts except you."

Lord Krishna answered, "Who performed good deeds in their lives, their souls never get ruined, neither in this world nor in the world after death. Their souls do not fall into evil."

"Those souls pass many years in heaven or in other holy worlds. Then they take birth again in wealthy and prosperous families.

Or, they are even born in the families of knowledgeable devotees instead of going to heaven. Such reincarnations are very difficult to obtain."

"Having enough good deeds from the past lives, they are gifted with enormous intelligence. In the present births, they try again more perfectly to attain the liberation of their souls.

They carried the habits of devotions from the previous births. Thus, as time goes on, they become unknowingly attracted towards the devotion to Paramatma. Although they may take births in prosperous families, their devotions destroy all the desirous thoughts from their minds."

"A true devotee destroys all sins in his present life, and it happens due to the effect of their earned good deeds from his previous lives. Thus, his soul certainly achieves its liberation in his present birth."

"A devotee is superior among a sage, a religious teacher and a man of action. Dear Arjuna, try to become a true devotee.

A person will be considered to be a great devotee, who always devotes to me with his pure and respectful mind."

Chapter Seven
The Path of Knowledge and Judgement

Lord Krishna said, "Dear Arjuna, now I am telling you the process, how you can know through your complete devotion that I am the supreme consciousness (the Paramatma).

I am enlightening your mind with this knowledge and by knowing this, no other knowledge will be left for you to know further."

"A few people try to know me among the thousands of people on the earth, and perhaps one among them becomes successful at last."

"The Maya (the material world) or nature is made of eight elements, earth, water, fire, air, space, mind, senses, and egoism. These are the materialistic nature of mine. Beyond the materialistic world, there is another form of mine, the ultimate consciousness, into which the entire universe is sustained."

"Dear Arjuna, all beings are created from both these materialistic and conscious nature. I am the ultimate reason for their creation and destruction."

"There is nothing superior to me. As precious stones are woven in a thread, the whole universe is woven inside me."

"Dear Arjuna, I am the liquidity in water; I am the shinning of the sun and moon; I am the '*Aum*' in Vedas; I am the sound in space; and I am the masculinity in human beings."

"I am the holy fragrance of earth; I am the heat of fire; I am the energies of all devotees."

"Dear Arjuna, I am the seeds of all lives; I am the intelligence of all intelligent persons; I am the strength of all powerful men."

"I am the abilities of humans; I am the required love for reproductions."

"Different effects are produced from three different qualities of humans' nature; These three qualities are known as, Good, Passion and Darkness (Sattva, Rajas and Tamas). Dear Arjuna, I am the creator of those three effects. However, I am free from those qualities and their effects."

"People are unable to escape from the delusion created by these three qualities. Thus, they do not know my eternal nature, by attaining beyond those qualities."

"The Maya is my creation, and it is difficult to comprehend. Only those people, who always devote to me, are able to escape from the world of illusion and to achieve liberation (Moksha)."

"Those people, who have lost their senses, and they become demonic, sinful, foolish and bad-hearted, do not devote to me."

"Dear Arjuna, only four types of people devote to me. They are seekers of truth, knowledgeable, poor, and seekers of wealth."

"Among them, only knowledgeable devotees are greatest. They are dear to me and also I am dear to them."

"My all devotees are good, but knowledgeable devotees are like me. They are true image of myself. They live inside me."

"Knowledgeable people achieve their present lives after many births and deaths. In the last birth, they worship me by knowing the truth that everything is me. These knowledgeable births are very rare to get."

"Many people have lost their senses due to their desirous thoughts. They eagerly follow their own rituals and worship demigods."

"I make their beliefs steady to their own gods in spite of having their desirous cause."

"They ultimately get their desired results but they do not know that they are actually getting their benefits from me."

"However, their desired results are temporary; everything vanishes as soon as they die. People who worship demigods, get their respective places with those gods, but those who devote to me, get their places with me."

"Ignorant people are unaware of the supreme nature of mine. They think that I am similar to other ordinary people."

"I do not reveal my true identity to others. I stay uncovered near to them by the Maya. Thus, they are unable to know that I am the supreme being, Paramatma. Near to them, I am a mortal and ordinary person."

"Dear Arjuna, I am completely aware of all happenings in the past, present, and future; but ignorant people never try to know me that way."

"All human beings have lost their senses due to the delusion produced from their joy and sorrow, desire and jealousy."

"However, those people who have abolished their sins by performing good deeds, become free from the delusion of attachments and the opposition created by the anger and jealousy. They show complete devotion to me."

"They completely surrender to me in order to escape the process of aging and death, and they become aware of spirituality and eternity (the ultimate destination of the soul). They are known as Brahman."

"Those people, who know me with Adhibhuta, Adhidaivya, and Adhiyogya (see next chapter), also know me at the time of their deaths, and they ultimately reach to me."

Chapter Eight
The Way to the Eternity

Arjuna asked, "Please explain me, what is Brahman (Paramatma)? What is spirituality? What is true action? What is Adhibhuta and what is Adhidaiva?"

"Who is Adhijogya and how does he live in our bodies? How do those devotees experience you just before their deaths?"

Lord Krishna said, "The supreme consciousness existing beyond this materialistic world is known as Brahman (Paramatma). The soul inside every living body is known as spirituality. The performed action without any material desire is known as true action."

"All materialistic mortal objects made of air, fire, water, earth, and space (void) are known as Adhibhuta. The first supreme lord who was created from the Paramatma, who created the universe, is known as Adhidaiva. And I am the Adhijogya who lives inside every being as his soul."

"The person, who leaves his body in a condition of remembering my true self at his last moment of life, ultimately reaches to me."

"Dear Arjuna, the state of mind before anyone's death leads him to his desired place after his death. Because, he always used to think in his lifetime about that state, consciously or subconsciously."

"You should always think about me and do your battle. If you surrender yourself to me through your mind and senses, doubtlessly you will attain my true self Paramatma."

"Because, the person, who always devotes to the supreme consciousness, Paramatma, with his concentrated mind, must attain the Paramatma after his death."

"The person, who is aware of everything, who is stable minded, who is the controller of all, who is modest, who is self-luminous, who is beyond ordinary senses, who is free from ignorance, and who is the keeper of all, is the devotee of the supreme Paramatma."

"During the death, the meditating devotee, by the power of devotion, put his soul between his two eyes, and he thinks about Paramatma with his concentrated mind. Ultimately, he achieves the supreme being, Paramatma."

"Vedic (follower of Vedas) sages describe the Paramatma as the syllable '*Aum*'. Sometimes, desireless devotees leave their families in order to achieve the Paramatma. Now I am stating you the way of achieving Paramatma."

"When a meditating devotee is dying, he is able to leave his body by controlling all the organs, setting the mind to the heart, fixing his life-air at the head, devoting himself to the Paramatma, chanting the word '*Aum*', thinking of my eternal self. That way he can reach to the Paramatma (Moksha)."

"I am easily attainable for those people who devote to me by always remembering me in his mind."

"Those people, who achieve their liberations (Moksha) once, do not return back to the sorrowful world again."

"The entire mortal universe also passes through the cycle of creation and destruction like the birth and death cycle of a soul. But, achieving me, one does not fall in the cycle of lives and births again. Because, the Paramatma is eternal, but the universe (Maya) is mortal."

"One thousand times of four *Yugas* in the human world is one day of Brahma. That amount of time is also equal for his one night."

"The whole universe emerges from the darkness at the day time of Brahma, and when night comes, the universe annihilates again to the darkness."

"All beings in this universe are created in the daytime and destroy at the night of Brahma. When the day comes again, the universe becomes alive."

"Beyond the cycle of creation and destruction, another eternity exists, who is the supreme Paramatma. Everything can be annihilated, but he is not."

"The supreme Paramatma is inexhaustible. The eternal unperceived Paramatma is the ultimate fate of every soul. Who archives him, never returns back. That is my divine form."

"All material worlds including this universe are sustained in the Paramatma. Only true devotion can lead to that state."

"Dear Arjuna, now I shall declare you the two different moments of death, one of which leads to the Moksha, and other leads to the cycle of birth and death."

"If someone passes away at the moment when the surface of the earth is brightened by all means, for example, at the daytime, the sun should rise at the northern solstice for six months, the moon should be at its bright fortnight etc., the person achieves the liberation."

"On the other hand, if someone passes away at the darker stage of earth, for example, the sun is at its southern solstice, the moon is at its dark fortnight, and at the night time, the person falls to the cycle of lives and deaths."

"Because, there are two paths, bright and dark. One path leads to the Paramatma, and another path leads to the cycle of lives and deaths."

"The person who knows the secret of these two paths, never shows any attachment. Dear Arjuna, you should also follow the brighter path and devote to me to achieve your liberation (*Moksha*)."

"All knowledgeable devotees follow the path of liberation through practicing sacred rituals, sacrifice, doing meditation and donation, thus certainly their good deeds cross all the barrier to his path of liberation."

Chapter Nine
The Secret and Mysterious Knowledge

Lord Krishna said, "I am again describing you the mysterious and secret knowledge leading to the path of Paramatma. Learning it, you will be liberated from the miserable material world."

"This knowledge is greatest among all other secret knowledge and education. It is very pure; It is superior; It is beneficial; It is easy to do; and it is eternal."

"Dear Arjuna, the person who is deviated from this devotional path, is unable to reach me. Eventually, he stays in the cycle of birth and death."

"The material world (the universe) is sustained in my unperceived form, the Paramatma. But, I am not sustained in this material world."

"See my divine power. Although I am the creator and protector of the material world, still my true-self does not live in this material world."

"As the wind is supported by the sky, similarly, all the material universe is supported by me."

"At the end of a *Kalpa* (one day of Brahma is one Kalpa), the entire universe submerges into me, and when another *Kalpa* starts, I create the universe again."

"As the universe and all beings maintain their own nature, following their natural laws, I create them again and again according to their actions."

"Those actions are unable to bind me because I am unattached and neutral."

"Under my supervision, the nature creates the whole universe, and the universe shows its own cycle of creation and annihilation."

"Ignorant people are unaware of my divine form, and they consider me as an ordinary human being. They sometimes ignore me unknowing the fact that I am the supreme Paramatma, descended in human form to rescue the world."

"Hopeless, actionless and unintelligent ignorant people are driven by their demonic and evil minds."

"But, godlike people with great souls know my eternity and divinity, and they always show their devotion to me through their great minds."

"Concentrating their minds only to me, they devote, worship and bow down to me, and they continuously chant my name and glorify me in order to achieve their liberations."

"Some people sacrifice to me through their knowledge. Some people worship me considering me as the unperceived Paramatma. And many other people worship me in their own ways such as worshipping idols."

"I am the Vedic rituals; I am the sacrifice; I am the offerings to gods; I am the medicinal herbs; I am the chanted verses; I am the extracted butter from milk; I am the fire; and I am the act of worshipping gods."

"I am the maintainer of the universe; I am the effects of actions; I am the father; I am the mother; I am the grandsire; I am the knowledge; I am the purity; I am the sacred syllable '*Aum*'; and I am the Rig, Sama, Yajur Vedas."

"I am the ultimate destiny; I am the protector; and I am the lord of all. I am the judge of good and bad; I am the shelter for all; I am the well-wisher; I am the reason of creation and destruction; I am the resting place of all the creations; I am the collector of seeds of life."

"I am the heat of sunbeam; I create rain from water; I am the eternity and death; and I am the soul and matter."

"Desirous people worship me following their religious literatures and through sacrifices to achieve the happiness of heaven. Due to their good deeds, they indeed attain heavenly happiness."

"However, that stage is temporary. When their good deeds become neutralized by the enormous enjoyments in heaven, they return back to this world again. Desirous people always go to heaven and return back to earth, thus they maintain the cycle of birth and death."

"But, who devote to me desirelessly, I bear all their deficiencies and preserve their efforts what they already have."

"Dear Arjuna, who worship other gods and goddesses, they are actually worshipping me (the Paramatma). But, their devotions are filled with ignorance."

"I am the ultimate recipient and lord of all sacrifices. Those who do not know my true for, fall into the cycle of birth and death."

"Worshippers of gods reach to the world of god; worshippers of ancestors reach to the world of ancestors; worshippers of ghosts reach to the world of ghosts and spirits; and worshippers of me reach to me and never take birth again."

"Who undesirously worships me with leaves, flowers, fruits, and water, I gladly receive his offerings."

"Dear Arjuna, you should also offer me your actions, your foods, your sacrifices, your donations, and your devotions."

"Renouncing all your actions to me, you will be free from all your attachments to those actions, and thus you will be rewarded your liberation."

"I exist everywhere; no one is my dear or hated to me. But, who show their devotions to me, I live in their hearts."

"Even, if any sinful person shows his devotion to me, he should be also known as a noble person, because his intention is pure."

"Soon he will be a righteous person, and he will find peace. Be sure, my devotees never degrade at any means."

"Anyone (irrespective of their castes, sexes, birth origins etcetera) takes shelter in me, and achieves his liberation. You should also devote to me by your mortal human form."

"Thus, there should not have any question for pure-hearted people; definitely, they will achieve liberation following my described paths. So, dear Arjuna, you should bow down to me and surrender your soul to me in order to attain me."

Chapter Ten
Endless Glories and Divinities of the Supreme

Lord Krishna said, "Dear Arjuna, you should again listen to my speech which is full of mystery and effectiveness. I am revealing the secret to you because you are my friend and I am your well-wisher."

"Gods or sages, no one knows the origin of my existence, because I am the eldest of all."

"Those desireless people eventually become free from all their sins knowing the fact that I am the unborn, the ancient and the sustainer of all creations."

"Power of justice, proper knowledge, intelligence, forgiveness, truthfulness, control of organs, mind control, joy and sorrow, creation and destruction, bravery and fear, nonviolence, equanimity, satisfaction, devotion, charity, fame and dishonor – all these states are evolved from me."

"Seven great sages, four ancient *Sanakas*, fourteen *Manus* - all of them possess the states of mine. And the whole population had been created from them."

"The person who knows my divinity with his proper knowledge, no doubt, is a follower of the path of devotion."

"I am the sole reason for all creations. The cycle of creation and destruction evolved from me. The knowledgeable person who knows all these truths, exclusively devotes to me considering me as my true self the Paramatma."

"Contended with their souls and minds by me, my devotees always get mental satisfaction through their conversation with themselves about my glories and divinities."

"I reward those devotees by delivering proper knowledge. Since they are always showing their devotions on me with the meditated mind, I deliver them the proper path through which they can reach to me."

"As a candle remove the darkness, my delivered knowledge removes their ignorance."

"Arjuna said, "You are the supreme Paramatma; you are the destiny; you are the purest; you are everywhere; you are eternal; you are unborn; you are divine and ancient. *Narada* (divine sage) and other sages described you in the same way. And you also described yourself the same."

"Dear Krishna, I accept the truth what you have said to me. Gods or demons, no one realized about your present incarnation."

"You are the lord of all beings; you are the god of all gods; you are the owner of the universe; you are the supreme. No one else knows you better than yourself."

"Everywhere is surrounded by your divinities. Only you can able to describe those divinities."

"O my supreme, please tell me how can I know you more? How should I train my mind with your thought?"

"Dear Krishna, tell me again about all your divinities and powers. I cannot help but listen to your words."

Lord Krishna said, "Dear Arjuna, I shall describe you some of my essential divinities because there is no end of my divinities."

"Dear Arjuna, I am the soul inside every being. I am the origin, midst and end of everything."

"I am the *Vishnu* among twelve sons of *Aditi* (mother of gods). I am the light of the sun among all lights. I am the *Marichi* among forty-nine *Vayus*. And I am the moon among the celestial bodies."

"I am *SamaVeda* among four Vedas. I am the *Indra* among all gods. I am the sense organs among all organs. I am the consciousness in a living body."

"I am the *Shankara* among eleven *Rudras*. I am the *Kuber* among all *Rakshasas* and *Yakshas*. I am the *Agni* (fire) among eight *Vasus*. I am the mountain *Sumeru* among all mountains."

"I am the *Brihaspati* among all sages. I am the *Kartikeya* among all commanders. I am the ocean among all water reservoir."

"I am the *Vrigu* among all great sages. I am the '*Aum*' among all sounds. I am the chanting of verses in religious rituals. And I am the *Himalaya* mountain among all immovable things."

"I am the *Ashvatta* tree (sacred fig) among all trees. I am the *Narada* sage among all heavenly sages. I am the *Chitrarath* among all *Gandharvas*. I am sage *Kapila* among all *Siddhas* (one who has reached his spiritual perfection)."

"I am the *Ucchaihshrava* (a divine horse who rose from the ocean during the collection of the elixir of immortality) among all horses. I am the *Airavata* (heavenly elephant) among all elephants. And I am the king among all humans."

"I am the *Vajra* (thunder) among all weapons. I am the *Kamadhenu* among all sacred cows. I am the love which is required to produce offspring. I am the king of snakes, *Vasuki* among all snakes."

"I am the king of serpents, *Ananta* among all serpents. I am the *Varuna* among all water gods. I am the *Arjama* among all ancestors. I am the god *Yama* (the god of death) among all concluders."

"I am the *Prahlada* among all demons. I am the time among all quantities. I am the lion among all animals. And I am the *Garuda* among all birds."

"I am the *Vayu* (wind) among all quick movers. I am the *Rama* among all soldiers. I am the *Makara* among all water animals."

"I am the origin, middle and end of the entire creation. I am spiritual knowledge among all knowledge. I am the concluder of truth among logicians."

"I am the first letter 'A' in alphabets. I am the conjunction in compound sentences. I am the endless time. And I am the Brahma among the creators."

"I am the death. I am the reason of creation that yet to be created. I am the seven qualities of women (fame, prosperity, polite speaking, memory, intelligence, courage, and forgiveness)."

"I am the *Brihatsama* among hymns. I am the *Gayatri* among poetic rhythms. I am the month *Agrahayan* (from mid of November to mid of December) among all months. I am the spring among seasons."

"I am the trickery in gambling. I am the glory and victory. I am the inspiration. I am the good qualities in virtuous people."

"I am the Krishna in the descendants of *Vrishni*. I am Arjuna among the *Pandavas*. I am the *Vedavyasha* among the religious authors. I am *Shukracharya* among the poets."

"I am the power of justice. I am the righteous way to achieve victory. I am the silence to keep something secret. I am the knowledge of all knowledgeable people."

"I am the reason for the existence of life on earth. No living body can get its consciousness except my consent."

"Dear Arjuna, as I said, there is no limit of my divinities. I described some of them to you."

"When you see something glorious, magnificent, beautiful in your surroundings, be sure, these are originated from me."

"There is no need to know them all. I am the sustainer of the whole universe and I maintain it by a small portion of my energy."

Chapter Eleven
Visioning the Supreme

Arjuna said, "O dear lord Krishna, I am feeling attachment-less and delusion-less after listening to your enlightening and mysterious speech."

"I have learned all the secrets about the creation and destruction of all beings. Also, I have enlightened by knowing your all divinities elaborately."

"O supreme, the ultimate truth what you have delivered, is enough for me. Now, I wish to see your supreme form filled with your divinities."

"Please show me your supreme and true form, if you consider me as an eligible person."

Lord Krishna said, "Dear Arjuna, behold my true identity, my cosmic form. In it, you will see my hundreds and thousands of divine forms of many shapes, sizes, and colors."

"Here you will see twelve *Adityas* (sons of *Aditi* who is the mother of gods), eight *Vasus*, eleven *Rudras*, *Ashwini Kumars* (twin god) and forty-nine *Vayus*. And you will see many others that you have never seen before."

"You can see the whole universe inside my divine body. And you will see many divinities that you wish to see."

"But, you will not be able to see my cosmic form with your human eyes. I am giving you divine vision to your eyes. Now, see my divine form with your divine eyes."

Then, lord Krishna showed his divine and infinite form to Arjuna.

In this divine form, Arjuna saw there were many faces and many eyes. The supreme form was magnificent to see. He was decorated with many divine ornaments, garlands, weapons, and garments. He was surrounded by heavenly fragrance. He was endless. He was amazing. His faces were everywhere.

He was shining as the thousand suns in the sky. Perhaps, a thousand suns were a lot dimmer than his divinity. Arjuna saw the whole universe is situated in a portion of his divine body.

Arjuna was in full wonder. The divine body of lord Krishna gave him goosebumps. Arjuna folded his hand and bowed his head and showed devotion to the supreme lord and said, "O lord Krishna, I am seeing all the gods and demons together. I am seeing lord Brahma and lord Shiva seated there. I am seeing all the sages and divine serpents situated there."

"I am seeing your vastness with infinite arms, infinite bodies, infinite eyes, and infinite faces. I cannot see your origin, middle, and end."

"I am seeing many weapons in your many hands. You are shining like fire and the sun. You became a source of infinite energy. You are beyond human perception."

"You are the supreme Paramatma. You are the only knowledge. You are the shelter of all beings. You are the keeper of truth. You are the eternal and divine person."

"I am seeing you as origin, mid and endlessly. You are the source of endless energy. I am seeing you as, you have many hands, the sun and moon in your eyes, your mouth is like a burning fire. you are maintaining the universe with your endless power."

"Everywhere is surrounded by you. You are the space between heaven and earth. The entire universe is frightening, beholding your extraordinary and unperceivable form."

"All are sheltering inside you. Many of them are praising to you with fear. Many sages and others are chanting hymns to get rescue from fear."

"Eleven *Rudras*, twelve *Adityas*, eight *Vasus*, all gods, *Gandharvas*, demons, and many others are seeing your divinities with their amazed visions."

"The whole universe and also me are frightening by seeing your many faces, many eyes, many arms, many legs, many bodies, and many teeth."

"I am not finding any peace but frightening by seeing your vastness touching to the sky. I am frightened by seeing your enormous mouth, your burning eyes, your energies, and many colors."

"I have lost my senses and lost my peace by seeing the burning fire emerging from your mouth. Your deformed teeth are frightening me as well. Please show mercy on me."

"Many warriors like Bhishma, Dronacharya, Karna and hundred Kaurvas are going into your enormous mouth. Many of their skeletons are hanging from your big teeth."

"As like river water meets to the ocean with its enormous speed, they are entering in your mouth with such enormous speed."

"As insects fall into the fire to die, they are also entering in your mouth to die."

"You are licking their blood with your tongue. O supreme being, you are frightening the entire universe by your endless energies."

"Please tell me, who are you in this dreadful form? I bow down to you. Be pleased. I wish to know you entirely. I am completely unaware of your intentions."

Lord Krishna in his cosmic form replied, "I am the time and death. I am eager to kill people. Most of your enemies will be dead in this war. It does not matter whether you will take part in this war or not."

"So dear Arjuna, rise for the battle and attain your fame. Enjoy enormous prosperity. I have already killed your enemies. You become merely the cause of their deaths."

"I have already killed many of the soldiers like Bhishma, Dronacharya, Karna, Jayadrath etcetera. You have to kill them who have been already killed. Do not be frightened. You must attain the victory. So, fearlessly do your battle."

Listening those words, Arjuna bowed down to lord Krishna with his shivering body and said with his frightened voice, "All beings rejoice by talking about your glories and they bow down to you, and all the frightened demons flee away from you – all these are now very much significant to me."

"You are the ancestor of the lord Brahma. you are infinity. You are the god of all gods. You are the maintainer of the universe. You are the both, sensible and beyond sensible. And above all, you are the supreme Paramatma. Why would not the devote to you."

"You are the origin of all. You are the ultimate shelter of all beings. You are both, the distributor of knowledge and the subject of knowledge. You are the ultimate destiny. You are the infinity who surround the entire universe."

"You are the *Vayu* (the god of wind). You are the *Yama* (the god of justice and death). You are the *Agni* (the god of fire). You are the *Varuna* (god of water). You are the *Chandra* (god of the moon). You are the creator *Brahma*, and you are the father of the *Brahma* also. I bow down to you a thousand times. I bow down to you again and again."

"I bow down to you from your front side. I bow down to you from your behind. I bow down to you from every side. The entire universe lies within you. Nothing is there beyond your abilities. You are the form of everything."

"Being my friend, many times I bullied you or dishonored you. I have done many mistakes to you knowingly or unknowingly. Please forgive all my mistakes. I beg mercy from you."

"You are the father of all beings. You are the person of respect. You are the person of influence. You are the master of all masters. No one is comparable to you. No one can be superior to you."

"So, I bow down to you again, and I praise you for your grace. As a father forgives his son, as a friend forgives his friend, and as a husband forgives his beloved wife, following the same, you forgive my all offenses."

"I have never seen such unimaginable supreme form. I am feeling joy by seeing this. And also I am trembling with fear. So, please return back to your previous form. Show me your eye soothing four-armed divine appearance."

"Please take the appearance to your four-armed form, wearing your divine crown on your head, holding your divine weapons in your hands."

Lord Krishna said, "I am pleased to you, thus I showed you my infinite, divine and energetic cosmic form. No one has seen this before, except you."

"In this material world, no one is able to see my cosmic form by any means. Any good deed, such as chanting sacred hymn, sacrifice, charity, sacred ritual or devotion is not enough for someone to compel me to transform into this divine form. You are the luckiest fortunate person to see this."

"Dear Arjuna, do not be afraid by seeing this, or do not behave like an ignorant. You should keep your fear away and behold my four-armed form again in your relaxed mood."

Then, lord Krishna transformed his appearance from the dreadful cosmic form to four-armed divine form.

He was holding, conch shell, *Sudarshana Chakra* (a disc-shaped weapon), Gada (a weapon) and lotus flower in his four hands. Seeing this peaceful appearance, Arjuna's fear was suppressed. Thereafter, he returned back to his mortal human form.

Arjuna said, "O lord Krishna, now seeing your peaceful form, my all fears have gone. My mind becomes stable again."

Lord Krishna said, "Dear Arjuna, my four-armed form that you have seen just now, is rare to see. Even all gods are eager to see it."

"And my supreme cosmic form is extraordinary. No one is able to see this even with his sacrifices, charities, sacred rituals, and penance."

"Only extreme devotion can lead my devotees to know my divinities thus they become eligible to see this form. There is no other way to achieve this rare state."

"Dear Arjuna, the person who devotes me through all his capabilities, who dedicates all his actions to me, who becomes desire-less and attachment-less, can achieve such state, and his soul reaches to me when he leaves the earth."

Chapter Twelve
The Path of Devotion

Arjuna asked, "Dear Krishna, many people worship your mortal human form. Whereas, many others devote directly to the structureless Paramatma. Which of them are considered to be the perfect devotees?"

Lord Krishna replied, "Dear Arjuna, people who devote to my human form, are considered to be the more perfect devotees. They should concentrate their mind to me with full respect, and they should consider me as the Paramatma in the human form."

"However, those people who devote directly to the structureless, eternal, beyond perception and all-pervading Paramatma with their steady and meditating minds and controlled organs, are also considered to be the perfect devotees. They also show the same equanimity to all beings. In the end, they will also meet me."

"But, showing devotion to the structureless Paramatma is hardest and painful practice to do. Because it is difficult to imagine structureless Paramatma for those people who are habituated in the world of manifestation."

"Those devotees who surrender all his actions on me, and perform their devotions through worshipping and meditation to my manifested human form, eventually get their rewards from me. They will get soon their liberation from this sorrowful earthly world."

"Dear Arjuna, you should fix your mind and senses to me. Doing so, you will doubtlessly attain your place into me."

"If you ever feel difficulty to concentrate your mind on me, there have other available ways. Then, you should practice devotion to me following easier methods."

"Even, if you ever fail to do so, do your works only for me. Thus, you can easily achieve your liberation."

"When you also fail to do this, you should try to control your mind and senses, and surrender all your actions to me. Doing this, you will also renounce your expectations from those actions."

"Dear Arjuna, knowledge is superior to practicing something without knowing anything about it. Performing meditation to the Paramatma is superior to knowledge. And renouncing all expectations from performed action is superior to meditation. Because renunciation can lead someone to the ultimate peace."

"Those devotees are dear to me, who do not feel jealousy to others, who are selfless, who are affectionate to all beings, who are merciful, who are free from ego, whose minds remain steady in sorrow and happiness, whose state of minds is always satisfied, who are self-controlled, who steadily devote their minds and senses on me."

"That person is my dearest devotee, who does not agitate someone, or who is not agitated by someone, who does not feel pain in other's happiness, who is free from joy and sorrow, fear and distress."

"That person is my dearest devotee, who is attachment-less, who is pure from inside and outside, who is skillful, who is free from hypocrisy, who is free from fear, who does not perform desirous actions."

"That person is my dearest devotee, who does not feel joy by getting something preferable, or does not feel sorrow by getting something undesirable, who does not lament when he has lost something, who does not seek for desirous things, who renounced all his good or bad actions."

"That person is my dearest devotee, who shows equanimity to friend and enemy, honor and dishonor, hot and cold, joy and sorrow, who does not involve himself in any conflict, and who is attachment-less."

"That steady minded devotee is my dearest, who shows equanimity to praising and condemning, who is polite, who is always satisfied to what he gets already in his life, who is attachment-less to his home and family."

"Those respectable people who perform such duties through his steady minded devotions, are my dearest devotees."

Chapter Thirteen
Relation of the Soul to the Body and Nature

Arjuna asked, "Dear Krishna, I wish to know the meaning of the 'field' (*Kshetra*) and the 'knower of the field' (*Kshetragya*). What is '*Prakriti*' and what is '*Purusha*'? What is the purpose of this knowledge?"

Lord Krishna replied, "The body that is made of earthly matter, is called the 'field'. And the entity who knows the body completely, is known as the knower of the field."

"Dear Arjuna, the eternal soul residing inside everybody is a small part of mine. And the soul is known as the 'knower of the field'. Thus, I am the 'knower of the field' since I live inside all living bodies. The knowledge provides the capacity for someone to differentiate the 'field' and the 'knower of the field'."

"Now learn from me about the field and the reason for modification of the 'field'. You should also know how the 'knower of the field' influences the body. Listen from me in details."

"The knowledge about the 'field' and the 'knower of the field' has been described in many ways by ancient sages. Various sacred texts have properly described them."

"The 'field' or the body has the following constituents and their modifications – the five elements such as, air, fire, water, earth and void (space); its primary features are egoism, intelligence, senses, ten organs, mind, and the subjects of five sense organs i.e. sound, touch, vision, smell, and taste."

"The 'field' interacts with its surroundings by desire, jealousy, happiness, sorrow, the material body, consciousness, and different states of mind."

"The goal of knowledge is to gain some qualities in human beings. These qualities are, having no feeling of pride or ego, harmlessness to other creatures, capacity of forgiveness, simplicity in mind and speech, showing respect and devotion to elders, cleanliness in body and mind, self-control, calmness, having no desire of prosperity in this world or in the heaven, feeling no trouble to the process of birth, aging, disease, and death,"

"Having no attachment to spouse, children, home and wealth, equanimity of mind in happiness and sorrow, purity in character, showing devotion to me with concentrated mind, habit of living in deserted and holy place, keeping safe distance from desirous people,"

"Constant practice of spirituality, knowledge, and absolute truth, having the feeling of 'The Paramatma is everywhere'."

"These are the characteristics of knowledge. Opposite of these are known as ignorance."

"Now I shall tell you about the subject of knowledge which will lead to a person to happiness and peace – the manifestation and unmanifestation of the Paramatma."

"The supreme Paramatma is everywhere. He spreads his organs, his hands, legs, eyes, head, mouth, and ears in all directions. However, his organs are unmanifested. He pervades the entire universe."

"He enjoys all senses of organs yet he has not any of them. He is the maintainer of all. Although he is structureless, still he can percept everything."

"He lives inside and outside of all movable and non-movable objects. He himself is both moving and nonmoving. Being unperceivable, he is beyond comprehension. He is very near to the knowledgeable, and he is too far from the ignorant."

"He is not divisible, yet he appears as divided among all beings (as their souls). You should know the Paramatma also as the creator, sustainer, and destroyer."

"He is the radiations of all illuminations. He is beyond the darkness. He himself is the knowledge, and also the subject of knowledge. He can be achieved only through the enlightenment of knowledge. He lives inside the heart of every living being as unmanifested way."

"These are the insight of the 'field'. 'knower of the field', knowledge and the goal of knowledge. My devotees achieve my divine form through the goal of knowledge."

"Dear Arjuna, now listen from me about the *Prakriti* (the nature) and the *Purusha* (soul in the body). The *Prakriti* and *Purusha* both are eternal and ancient. The states of mind such as, anger, attachment, jealousy, and three different qualities (*Swattva, Rajasa, Tamasa*) are produced by the *Prakriti* (nature)."

"All the actions and causes occur due to the existence of *Prakriti*. The soul inside a body experiences happiness and sorrow because different effects arise due to the interaction of *Prakriti* with those actions and causes."

"The *Purusha* has to encounter all the effects that evolved from those three qualities (*Swattva, Rajasa, Tamasa*). Thus, the soul or the *Purusha* takes his birth in different wombs to suffer the outcome of his actions and the causes of actions."

"Every soul living inside every being is a part of the supreme Paramatma. He is the witness of all; he is the authority; he is the sufferer; he is the keeper and controller. Being unmanifested, he is the Paramatma."

"The person who completely knows the Purusha, Prakriti and the interaction between them due to those three qualities (*Swattva, Rajasa,*

Tamasa), never returns back to this material world again. He will achieve the liberation whatever be his present condition."

"Pure minded people try to manifest the Paramatma in their hearts following different pathways. Some people follow the path of meditation or devotion, others follow the path of knowledge, and many others follow the path of action."

"But, many ignorant people are unable to follow those paths, however, they try to listen about the Paramatma from various knowledgeable persons, and gathering that knowledge, they devote to the Paramatma, and ultimately attain their liberation from this sorrowful world."

"All the creatures from plants to animals are produced through the interaction of the 'field' and 'knower of the field'."

"The Paramatma lives equally inside all living beings – only true viewers know this fact."

"Since the true-viewers see the presence of Paramatma everywhere and inside every living being, they do not harm themselves or others. So, they are rewarded accordingly."

"Those people are true viewers who can visualize that every incident is happening by the *Prakriti* (nature), and there is no role of souls (*Purusha*)."

"They visualize the Paramatma as one single entity, who is showing different appearances in different bodies. They know the truth that every living body is showing its existence because of him.

At the end, these true-viewers will eventually meet to the Paramatma."

"Dear Arjuna, being unmanifested and eternal, the Paramatma is living inside everybody, yet he does not perform any action and never involves himself into any action."

"As space covers the entire universe, but it does not take part in the actions of the universe. Similarly, being unperceived, the soul never attaches to the qualities of the body."

"As the sun shines the surface of the earth, the soul shines the body (field)."

"Here I mentioned all the differences between the 'field' and 'knower of the field'. Also, I stated the instruction through which someone can get escape from the '*Prakriti*' and the actions of the *Prakriti*. The person who can realize the truth through his knowledge, eventually he will attain the Paramatma."

Chapter Fourteen
The Three Qualities

Lord Krishna said, "I shall declare you again the most perfect knowledge among all others. Following the path of that knowledge, many sages and saints have achieved their supreme goal."

"Followers of this knowledge never return back to the material world again, after achieving me. They do not tremble at the time of the destruction of the universe (apocalypse), and they cross the barrier of birth and death."

"Dear Arjuna, *Prakriti* is the womb of all living beings, and I put the life inside that womb. Thus, all lives are born as conscious beings. All lives are combinations of consciousness and material substances."

"Different types of living organisms are produced in the womb of *Prakriti*. Thus, *Prakriti* (nature) is the mother of those organisms, and I am their father."

"Dear Arjuna, three different qualities, *Swattva* (good), *Rajasa* (passionate) and *Tamasa* (dark), are responsible for the attachment of the soul to its body."

"*Swattva* or the good quality is superior to other two qualities. It is pure and illuminating, thus, it binds the soul with knowledge and happiness."

"*Rajasa* or the quality of passion arises from desires and attachments. This quality binds the soul with desirous actions."

"The third quality, *Tamasa* or the darkness arises from ignorance. It binds the soul with ignorance, laziness, and sleeping."

"Dear Arjuna, quality of goodness (*Swattva*) creates attachments to happiness and peace; quality of passion (*Rajasa*) creates attachments to desirous actions; and quality of darkness (*Tamasa*) creates attachments to ignorance fading the knowledge."

"Dear Arjuna, quality of goodness dominates over the quality of passion and darkness; quality of passion sometimes dominates over the quality of goodness and darkness; likewise, quality of darkness dominates over the quality of goodness and passion."

"The increase of good quality can be observed when the mind and senses are illuminated by knowledge."

"The signs of the quality of passion can be observed when it dominates over the two others. The signs are greediness, desire, desirous actions, jealousy, agitation in mind, attraction to earthly pleasure."

"When the quality of darkness increases, it shows laziness, ignorance, illusions, excessive sleeping."

"When a person of good quality dies, he gets an extraordinary place after his death."

"When a person dies with his passionate quality, his desires compel him to take birth again in this world."

"And when a person of dark quality dies, his soul is born again in the wombs of lower class creatures such as, insects, animals etcetera."

"The result of actions with good quality is pure happiness; the result of actions with passionate quality is sorrow; and the result of actions with dark quality is ignorance."

"Good quality produces knowledge; Passionate quality creates greediness; and dark quality creates ignorance, illusion and wrong actions."

"As I already said, the good quality leads to heaven, the passionate quality leads to birth in human world, and the dark quality leads to birth as lower class animals.

But, when a person realizes that all the actions are the results of these three qualities, and knows me as the unperceived Paramatma, he achieves my divinities."

"Realizing the fact that all these three qualities are associated with the body, and there is no role of the soul, he becomes free from the sorrowful cycle of birth, aging, disease and death. Thus, he achieves the ultimate peace."

Arjuna asked, "What are the characteristics of that person who has crossed the barrier of these three qualities? How does he behave? And what are the processes through which one can cross the barrier?"

Lord Krishna replied, "Dear Arjuna, the effect of good quality is illumination; the effect of passionate quality is desire; and the effect of dark quality is delusion and ignorance. But, the person who is free from these qualities, never hates or resists those qualities. He keeps his mind stable and never shows agitation to those qualities, by knowing the truth that those qualities are created by the Maya (the delusion). He concentrates his mind to the Paramatma and he never deviates from that state of mind."

"He stays stable to his soul. He shows equanimity of mind to sorrow and happiness. A piece of stone and a piece of gold are equally valueless near to him. Pleasant and unpleasant both are equal near to him. He shows equanimity to honor and dishonor. He acts neutrally to his enemy and friend. He accepts equally to blame and praise. He never boasts about his actions. Then, the person reaches to the state of beyond these qualities."

"The desireless person who devotes to me with his exclusive service, becomes also free from those qualities and he must achieve his liberation reaching to the Paramatma."

"Because I am the seldom basis of the Paramatma in human form. I am also the basis of elixir of eternity and endless happiness."

Chapter Fifteen
The Supreme Entity

Lord Krishna said, "Dear Arjuna, imagine an enormous banyan tree, which is eternal. Its primary root is the Paramatma. The sacred scripters, Vedas are its leaves. The lord Brahma is its stem. The person who knows the tree entirely, is known as the perfect knowledgeable."

"As an ordinary tree is nourished by water, similarly, that enormous eternal tree is also nourished by the three qualities (*Swattva*, *Rajasa* and *Tamasa*). Its branches are stretched upwards, downwards and all other directions. Those branches are considered as the living organisms, such as humans and other creatures. Its branches are extended further according to the qualities of those living organisms, that bind them to their actions, such as, ego, desires, affection etcetera."

"One cannot perceive the whole tree by his mind. The tree is vast, endless and eternal, eventually, someone is able to manifest only its outside. But the Paramatma is deeply-rooted inside beyond human manifestation. One should have to cut the tree by weapon to search for the Paramatma."

"The Paramatma is the ultimate destination; achieving him, a person never returns back to this world again. The whole tree is emerged from its root, *i.e.* from the Paramatma. One should take his shelter inside into it through his mind, soul and heart."

"The knowledgeable person, who has eliminated his attachments and desires, who is free from delusions and evils, whose mind is steadily concentrated to the Paramatma, who is not agitated by pleasure and pain, achieves that highest state."

"Once someone achieves this highest state, he gets his liberation, and never returns back to this sorrowful world."

"That state is my place. The sun, moon or fire are not able to illuminate that supreme, because that supreme Paramatma is itself illumination."

"All souls inside living bodies are my eternal parts. Inside the *Prakriti* (the nature), the soul is bound by mind and five other senses."

"As the wind transfers the fragrance of a flower from one place to another, similarly, the soul carries the mind and five senses from one body to other."

"The soul enjoys all the senses like vision, sound, smell, taste, and touch through the five sense organs (eyes, ears, nose, tongue, and skin) with the help of the mind."

"It is hard to perceive the soul for ignorant people when it resides inside the body, because those three qualities delude the mind. Only knowledgeable people are able to perceive the soul."

"Only knowledgeable people have the ability to perceive it. But ignorant people never realize the soul because their hearts and minds are not pure."

"The shining of the sun which is also the reason for illumination of the solar system, the moon, and the fire, also comes from me."

"I am the maintainer of the universe with my divine energy. I nourish the plant at night by the illumination of the moon."

"I created the digestive system for living beings, thus they obtain the required energies to live."

"I live inside everyone's heart. I am the reason of their memories, knowledge, and forgetfulness of bad happenings. I am the subject of knowledge from Vedas. I am also the author of Vedanta."

"There are two types of entities in the creation; these are mortal and eternal. All material bodies are mortal, whereas, souls are eternal."

"Different from these two, there is another kind of entity, who is the Paramatma. He is the sustainer and maintainer of the universe."

"Since I am different from everything, beyond mortality, even superior to the soul, thus I am also known as the supreme personality."

"The knowledgeable person who knows me as the supreme being, doubtlessly, always devotes to me."

"Dear Arjuna, Thus I declared you the mysterious and confidential knowledge. Knowing it, many people become educated and satisfied."

Chapter Sixteen
Demonic and Godlike Personalities

Lord Krishna said, "Two categories of people are there, godlike and demon-like. Godlike people have their own characteristics. They are fearless; their hearts and minds are pure; They practice meditation to gain more knowledge; they donate to other without any expectation in return; their minds and organs are self-controlled; they show respect to father, mother and other elders; they worship gods; they perform sacred rituals; they maintain their duties, even if those are painful to them; they keep simplicity in their hearts, minds, and senses."

"They do not hurt other beings; they talk politely; They talk politely; they do not hate others even to sinful persons also; they do not boast to their performed actions; their minds are stable and not agitated; they do not blame others; they are merciful to others. Although already having enough earthly pleasure, earthly pleasure and wealth, they do not attach to those. They feel pain when someone goes against a righteous path."

"They are illuminating, merciful, kind-hearted, full of patience; they are pure from outside and inside; they do not show enmity."

"On the other hand, demonic people are completely opposite in characters. Qualities of demon-like people are hypocrisy, arrogance, cruelty, anger, and ignorance."

"Qualities of godlike people lead to the liberation, whereas demonic qualities create an attachment to the deluded world (*Maya*). Dear Arjuna, you do not need to lament because you possess those godlike qualities."

"Dear Arjuna, as I said, two types of humans have been created by *Maya* (delusion). One category has godlike characters and another category has demonic characters. I have already described the characteristics of godlike people, now listen to the description of the characters of demonic people."

"Demonic people do not have the ability to judge the difference between right action and prohibited action. Thus, their minds and senses are impure; they do not perform righteous acts; and they are not truthful."

"They always say, there is no existence of right or wrong, all are equal. They do not believe in gods; they are dishonest and liars. They believe, all beings are created from sexual activity and there is no role of the god."

"These cruel-minded, ignorant, dishonest, misbehaving people are born to destroy the world."

"Occupied with desirous thoughts, hypocrisy, pride and arrogance, they follow harmful paths due to their ignorance. These dishonest misdirected people live in this society among others."

"They continue to think about earthly pleasure until their deaths, and they luxuriously live their lives with wealth and prosperity pretending that nothing could be happier than that."

"They bind themselves with various desires. Being deluded by anger and lust, they try to fulfil their desires following various unfair means."

"They continue to think that, at present, they have an enormous amount of wealth, and in the future, they have to get more."

"They think, they have defeated their enemy today, and they will eliminate more on tomorrow. They pretend themselves as they are god. They think that they are happy, they are powerful."

"They think, 'I am so much wealthy', I have so many friends and followers', 'Who can be happier than me?', 'I shall lead my life luxuriously'. But, ultimately those ignorant, desirous and deluded demonic people will be put into the hell."

"Imagining himself as the greatest, those arrogant, hypocrite and selfish people reluctantly sacrifice very minute quantity."

"Being deluded by arrogance, ego, desire, anger and power, they hate others. Behaving such, they are actually hating their souls and also hating me."

"I put those hateful, dishonest, cruel peoples' souls in demons' wombs again and again.

"Dear Arjuna, those ignorant people never reach to me and they take births as demons. After taking many obnoxious births, they are put into hell."

"Desire, anger, and greed are the doors of hell, and these are the reasons for the degradation of a soul. One should avoid those qualities as poison."

"Only those people who are free from those three doors of hell, become successful for the welfare of their souls. They ultimately reach to me by achieving liberation."

"Those people, who have rejected instructions from sacred scriptures, and lead their lives with their desired wishes, never attain their liberation."

"Sacred scriptures dictate which action is righteous and which is not. So dear Arjuna, you should do your actions following those scriptures."

Chapter Seventeen
Way of Life

Arjuna asked him again, "Dear Krishna, some people do not follow sacred scriptures but they worship gods in their own way. However, they do not show deficiency in their devotions. In which category their devotions belong, good (*Swattvik*), passionate (*Rajasik*), or dark (*Tamasik*)."

Lord Krishna answered, "Dear Arjuna, every person has his own devotional path from his instinct. These devotional paths are *Swattvik, Rajasik,* and *Tamasik,* and those are outside from any sacred scriptures. Listen about those."

"Dear Arjuna, devotion comes from peoples' hearts. Humans' nature is devotional, so their devotions follow their inherent natures."

"People with good quality worship gods; people with passionate quality worship *Yakshas* and *Rakshasa*; and people with dark quality worship ghosts and spirits."

"Some people strongly worship gods to fulfill their desires and powers arose from ego and pride. The path of worship is completely outside of sacred texts. They are torturing their souls and also me (since I live in everyone's heart). Those ignorant people are known to be demon-like."

"Foods, sacrifices, and donations are also categorized into three qualities. Listen to their differences from me."

"People with good qualities (*Swattvik*) prefer those foods which are nutritious, tasteful and juicy. Those foods increase life span, strength, intelligence, happiness, and health."

"People with passionate quality love to eat bitter, salty, sour, very hot, pungent, spicy and dry foods. Those foods increase sadness, disease, and anxiety."

"People with dark quality prefer to eat impure, stinky, stale and half-cooked foods."

"Sacrifices should be always done by following the sacred texts. Such sacrifices which are done by people without any desire, are known as *Swattvik* (good) sacrifices."

"But dear Arjuna, people also perform sacrifices from their pride and to accomplish their desires. Those sacrifices are known as *Rajasik* (passionate) sacrifices."

"Some people also perform sacrifices without following the sacred literatures, without donation of foods, without chanting sacred verses, and without showing devotion. Those sacrifices are known as *Tamasik* (dark) sacrifices."

"Showing respect to gods, to teachers, to knowledgeable persons, and to Brahmins (knower of Brahma or Paramatma), maintaining simplicity, purity, nonviolence in lifestyle, are known as penance through the body."

"Practicing non-distressful, truthful, polite and beneficial speeches, chanting of verses from *Vedas* and in the name of gods, are known as penance through speech."

"Penances through minds are maintaining purity in mind, self-control of mind, thought of Paramatma, and maintaining a peaceful and concentrated mind."

"These penances are when performed by desireless people through their body, speech and mind, are known as *Swattvik* (good) penance."

"When penance in order to gain honor, respect, and to fulfill self-desire, the penance is likely to be unsuccessful and effects are transient. Such penance is known as *Rajasik* (passionate) penance."

"When penance is performed in order to achieve impossible, having the desire to harming others, through torturing own health, such penance is called *Tamasik* (dark) penance."

"Charity (donation) is a wise duty. When charity is performed in a sacred place, at the perfect time, to the needful people, and without any desire of anything in return, then the charity is known as *Swattvik* charity (good)."

"When a charity is reluctantly performed by someone to get benefit from it, the charity is known as *Rajasik* (passionate) charity."

"When charity is donated to unworthy persons, without showing respect, in improper place, and at a wrong time, such charity is known as Tamasik (*dark*) charity."

"The supreme Paramatma has been symbolized by the term '*Aum Tath Sath*'. Through these three syllables, before the creation of the universe, the performer of sacrifice has been represented by Brahmin (knower of the Brahma or Paramatma); the medium of sacrifice has been specified by *Vedas*; and the deed has been specified by the sacrifice."

"Following the sacred scriptures, someone should start his sacrifice, penance or charity by chanting '*Aum*' (which is the symbol of Paramatma)."

"The performer non-desirably performs sacrifice, penance, and charity by chanting the second syllable '*Tath*'."

"The third syllable symbolizing the Paramatma, '*Sath*' is used to describe purity and goodness."

"The actions that are performed in sacrifice, penance, and charity in the name of Paramatma, is also denoted by '*Sath*'."

"Dear Arjuna, the actions such as sacrifice, penance, and charity when performed without showing respect and in an impure condition, the actions are called '*Asath*'. Such actions have no effect in this world and also in the world after death."

Chapter Eighteen
Liberation and Renunciation

Arjuna said again, "Dear Krishna, I wish to know more about renunciation. Please explain to me the difference between 'renunciation' (*Tyaag*) and 'practicing true renunciation' (*Sannyaas*)."

Lord Krishna said, "Knowledgeable people say that renunciation of all types of actions including necessary actions in life is known as 'practice of true renunciation' (*Sannyaas*). On the other hand, they also say that renunciation of all desires from the performed actions is known as 'renunciation' (*Tyaag*)."

"Some knowledgeable people say, all types of actions are imperfect so one should renounce all actions. But other knowledgeable people say, one should not renounce all actions rather he should perform virtuous actions such as sacrifice, penance, and charity."

"Dear Arjuna, you should learn about both, 'renunciation' and 'practicing true renunciation'. At first, I shall tell you about 'renunciation' (*Tyaag*). Listen from me. Three types of renunciations are there, good (*Swattvik*), passionate (*Rajasik*) and dark (*Tamasik*)."

"One should not renounce virtuous actions, such as sacrifice, penance, and charity. Rather, one should perform those actions properly. Because those virtuous actions are the required actions for intelligent persons."

"In my well-determined opinion, all those virtuous actions and other actions must have to be done without any desire and attachment."

"One should not renounce necessary and useful actions. Because necessary actions are required for the purity of mind. Renunciation of necessary actions due to delusion is known as dark renunciation (*Tamasik Tyaag*)."

"Some people renounce their necessary actions thinking that actions are painful and sorrowful. Such renunciation is known as passionate renunciation (*Rajasik Tyaag*). One will not achieve liberation (*Moksha*) performing those renunciations."

"Dear Arjuna, performing actions following sacred scriptures is a duty. One should perform those action renouncing all the desires and attachments. Such renunciation of desire and attachment in actions is known as good renunciation (*Swattvika Tyaag*)."

"The intelligent and doubtless person who does not hate inferior actions and does not attach to superior actions, is known as good renouncer (Swattvik)."

"It is impossible to renounce all actions for a person. However, a perfect renouncer renounces all desires from his performed actions."

"Some people fail to renounce their desires from actions. They have to bear three types of effects, good, bad and combination of good and bad after their deaths. But, those people who renounced desires from their actions, do not bear any effect of actions after death."

"Dear Arjuna, there are five elements which are responsible for actions. There have also some ways which can lead someone to renounce all attachments of actions. Listen about those ways from me."

"These five elements of action are the body, the performer, various senses, various efforts, and divinities (without god's will, an action could not be accomplished)."

"These are the five causes through which people accomplish the proper or improper actions with their body, senses, and speeches."

"In spite of the fact, some people think due to their ignorance that the soul is the seldom performer of actions. They misunderstand the soul."

"Intelligent persons never show the mentality, 'I am the performer of action'. Their minds and senses are free from desire of earthly materials and attachments of actions. If they ever mistakenly kill the entire population, they do not incur sin."

"Knowledge, the subject of knowledge and the knower are three producers of action. And, the performer of action, the instrument of action and the action itself are the three ingredients of action."

"According to philosophy, knowledge, action, and performer of action have been categorized by three qualities, good (*Swattva*), passionate (*Rajasa*) and dark (*Tamasa*). Listen from me about those qualities."

"The knowledge, through which someone realizes that the souls inside all living beings are one indivisible entity of the supreme soul Paramatma, is known as the knowledge of good quality (*Swattvika*)."

"The knowledge that leads to the delusion of individuality of every soul, is known as the knowledge of passionate quality (*Rajasik*)."

"The inappropriate knowledge which implements in the human mind that body is everything, and it creates attachments to bodily pleasure, is known as the knowledge of dark quality (*Tamasik*). The dark knowledge evolves from ignorance and imperfection."

"When an action is performed by someone following the direction given in the sacred text, through desire less, selfless and nonviolent way, the action is known as a good mode of action (*Swattvik*)."

"When an action is performed to fulfill desire, in an extremely painful way, and with ego, the action is known as a passionate mode of action (*Rajasik*)."

"When an action is performed by endless expenses of money and strength, to harm others, without aware of bad effect of the action and when the action is beyond the capability of the performer, the action is called dark mode of action (*Tamasik*)."

"When a performer of action does not feel happiness on his success, and does not feel sorrow on his failure, when the performer free from desire, selfishness, and ego, when he performs the action efficiently and patiently, then the performer is called a good performer (*Swattvik* performer)."

"When a performer performs his action with mindful of desires, greed, and impurity, when his action may harm others, when he feels the happiness of success and pain of failure, the performer is then called a passionate performer (*Rajasik* performer)."

"When a performer is distracted minded, completely ignorant, impolite, arrogant and lazy, when he keeps aside easier task for long term with intention of to be done later, when his mind is always unhappy, the performer is known as a performer of dark quality (*Tamasik* performer)."

"Dear Arjuna, intelligence and state of mind can also be categorized with respect to these three qualities. I am going to tell you about those differences."

"Dear Arjuna, the intelligence which assists the humans to differentiate between right action and wrong action, fear and no-fear, good and bad, and attachment and liberation, are known as the intelligence of good quality (*Swattvik*)."

"The intelligence which fails to differentiate righteous and wrong action, good and bad, what ought to be done and what ought to be not done, is known as the intelligence of passionate quality (*Rajasik*)."

"The intelligence which deludes human senses as bad is good and wrong is right, is known as the intelligence of dark quality (*Tamasik*)."

"Dear Arjuna, the state of mind which leads to someone to practice meditation thus he gains the purity of mind, soul and body, is known as the state of mind of good quality (*Swattvik*)."

"When a desirous minded person shows attachment towards wealth, desire and action through his thought, the state of mind is categorized in passionate quality (*Rajasa*)."

"The state of mind which compels someone not to renounce the habits of sleeping, distress, depression, and addiction, is known as the state of mind of dark quality (*Tamasa*)."

"Dear Arjuna, now listen from me the categorization of happiness also. The happiness which can be achieved through practicing meditation, devotion, and service (duties), is known as the happiness of good quality. This kind of happiness is able to purify mind such that someone is able to escape from all his sorrows. However, at the first stage, it tastes bitter, but the ultimate result is sweet."

"The happiness which arises from the interaction of organ to wealth, is known as the happiness of passionate quality. This kind of happiness appears as sweet at first, but the ultimate result is poisonous."

"When happiness deludes people and leads them to ignorance, is known as dark happiness. This kind of happiness arises from sleeping, laziness, and ignorance."

"In heaven or earth, there is no one who is free from these three qualities."

"Dear Arjuna, humankind is also categorized into four classes according to their qualities of actions and habits. Those classes are Brahmin, Kshatriya, Vaishya, and Sudra."

"Brahmins are those people who possess self-controlled minds and organs, who keep their minds and bodies pure, who have the quality of forgiveness to others, who maintain simplicity, who show respect to sacred scriptures and gods, who study sacred scriptures and who is a knower of the supreme soul Paramatma."

"Kshatriyas are those who are brave and strong, who are well skilled in weaponry, who do not retreat away from a battle, who perform charities and who have the power of justice."

"Vaishyas are those who have occupation of dairy, farming, and business. They should maintain honesty while dealing with others. And finally,

Sudras are those who serve the other three classes of people."

"Now listen from me the way, following that one can attain the liberation even being involved in his everyday actions. This is the way how one can easily devote to the Paramatma by doing his natural actions."

"His every day's natural actions then will be considered as his worshipping to the Paramatma (who is the creator of all and who pervades the entire universe)."

"Own natural actions are better than others' actions (however superior). Because, one will not incur sin when he performs his own action, in which he is habituated."

"So dear Arjuna, one should not abandon his own action, in spite of that the action is being defective. As fire is contaminated with its smoke, likewise every action is contaminated with its defect."

"Following the path of renunciation, such desireless, unattached, intelligent and self-controlled persons achieve the highest state renouncing all the effects from their actions."

"Dear Arjuna, know from me how someone archives the Paramatma following the path of knowledge through their inaction (the action which does not affect in karma)."

"A person is able to achieve the Paramatma following the specific paths. He should be a person of pure mind, good qualities (*Swattvika*) and controlled diet. He should live in a holy place. He should renounce all his attraction to wealth and earthly pleasures. His organs and mind should be well controlled by the good state of mind. He should abandon anger and hatred. He should practice meditation renouncing ego, desires, pride, anger, and power (feeling of being powerful due to ego). His mind should be stable and well concentrated. And finally, he should devote to the Paramatma."

"A completely devoted person to the Paramatma never keeps any desire or attachment in his mind, and also he does not feel sorrow. Ultimately, he achieves his reward from me."

"Those persons eventually know me through their complete devotion, and ultimately they reach to me."

"Moreover, those people who are the followers of the path of action, are also able to achieve the Paramatma through their desireless actions."

"Dear Arjuna, you should dedicate all your actions to me, and concentrate your mind and senses to me."

"Thus, you will be able to cross all the barriers from your path to my blessings. On the other hand, if you do not obey my advice due to your ego, you will deviate yourself from the path of Paramatma."

"You have determined that you will not participate in the war, but your determination is wrong, because your inherent nature will compel you to take participate in this battle."

"You are deviated from your action by your delusion, but your previous habits to your natural actions will compel you to continue your duties."

"Dear Arjuna, the delusion created by Maya is responsible to engage someone to his own actions. The supreme Paramatma lives inside every being as his soul, thus Paramatma is the only reason due to which every being is engaged in his own action."

"Dear Arjuna, you should also surrender to the Paramatma, thus you will achieve your ultimate peace by his blessings."

"Dear Arjuna, I declared the secret and mysterious knowledge to you. Now you should choose wisely your decision."

"This knowledge is most confidential of all secrets. I shall declare you the confidential and mysterious instruction again. I am revealing the beneficial instruction because you are my friend and very dear to me."

"Dear Arjuna, concentrate your mind to me, devote to me, worship me, and bow down to me. I swear, if you follow my suggestion, you will reach to me."

"You should surrender all your actions and duties to me, and take your shelter into me. Thus you will be free from all your sins, do not fear."

"You should not tell the mysterious knowledge to those people who are deviated from penance and devotion. You should not tell those who are unwilling to listen. And you should not tell those who are hateful to me."

"The person who declares the mysterious knowledge to my devotees, doubtlessly he will attain me.

That person is my dearest among all others devotees, and in future, no other devotee will not be dearer than him."

"The person who reads the sacred Bhagavad Gita, is actually worshipping me through his sacrifice of knowledge (see previous chapters)."

"The person who listens to the Bhagavad Gita with his devotional and pure mind, also becomes free from his sins and achieves me."

"Dear Arjuna, did you listen carefully to my instructions? Has your ignorance been removed listening to this?"

At last, Arjuna replied, "Dear Krishna, yes, my ignorance and delusion have gone away. I get back my memories. My all doubts have gone away. Thus, I must follow your instructions."

♦♦♦♦♦

The secret and mysterious conversation between Krishna and Arjuna had ended here. Sanjay was listening to the whole conversation, and he was narrating it to king Dhritarashtra. Vedavyasa had given him the capacity of distant vision to him. He was shivering with by listening to the extraordinary conversation. He was also excited by recalling the cosmic form of lord Krishna. Thus, he concluded to Dhritarshtra that no one was able to defeat a group of the armies, where lord Krishna and Arjuna took part.

Easy Bhagavad Gita

Printed in Great Britain
by Amazon